From One Father to Another

Dave,

May God show you how much He loves you through the love of your own children. God bless my friend.

What Becoming
a Father Taught Me
about God

From One Father to Another

KEVIN ROBERT JARVIS

FROM ONE FATHER TO ANOTHER
Copyright © 2020 by Kevin Robert Jarvis

All rights reserved. Neither this publication nor any part of this publication may be reproduced or transmitted in any form or by any means, electronic or mechanical, including photocopying, recording or any information storage and retrieval system, without permission in writing from the author.

Scripture marked AMPC taken from the Amplified® Bible, Classic Edition, Copyright © 1954, 1958, 1962, 1964, 1965, 1987 by The Lockman Foundation. Used by permission. • Scripture marked ESV taken from The Holy Bible, English Standard Version® (ESV®), Copyright © 2001 by Crossway, a publishing ministry of Good News Publishers. Used by permission. All rights reserved. • Scripture marked NIV taken from The Holy Bible, New International Version®, NIV® Copyright ©1973, 1978, 1984, 2011 by Biblica, Inc.® Used by permission. All rights reserved worldwide. • Scripture marked RSV taken from the Revised Standard Version of the Bible, copyright © 1946, 1952, and 1971 the Division of Christian Education of the National Council of the Churches of Christ in the United States of America. Used by permission. All rights reserved.

Printed in Canada

ISBN: 978-1-4866-1970-2
eBook ISBN: 978-1-4866-1971-9

Word Alive Press
119 De Baets Street Winnipeg, MB R2J 3R9
www.wordalivepress.ca

Cataloguing in Publication information can be obtained from Library and Archives Canada.

*This book is dedicated to my three wonderful children,
Owen, Kara, and Luke*

Acknowledgements

I WOULD NOT HAVE BEEN ABLE TO COMPLETE THIS BOOK without the love and support of my wife Jessica, who kept urging me to keep writing despite my doubts. I love you. My mother Sharon Collard was hugely instrumental in the publishing process, and I want to thank her with added emphasis.

I'm also indebted to my unofficial proofreaders, Holly Kirk Mclean and Micah Vandervaart, who suggested minor course corrections pertaining to content and provided plenty of encouragement for the overall worthiness of the book.

I cannot fail to mention the House of Shalom Youth Centre, where I was first introduced to God and where my greatest friendships began. The House has been a haven for many years, and greatly contributed to the person I am today.

I'm extremely grateful to my editors Stephanie Renaud and Matthew Knight. I would also like to acknowledge Sylvia St. Cyr and Marina Reis of Word Alive Press for their ongoing support and contribution to bringing this book through the publishing process and into readers hands.

A special thanks to Piero Amicone for agreeing to write the foreword of the book; you are a friend like no other.

Owen, Kara, and Luke, you have brought the most precious kind of love into my life, one more profound than I could have ever imagined. Without the three of you, this book absolutely could not exist. I am closer to God because of the love I'm blessed to share with each of you. I cannot think of anything in this world that compares to getting to be your dad. I love all three of you from the very depths of my heart.

Most importantly, I would like to thank the Lord Jesus Christ and God our Father. You have been by my side all the days of my life. You were with me as I walked my old neighbourhood streets seemingly alone, as well as the many times I was numb with grief, and even now as I walk further down the path you have planned for me. I love you and thank you for never leaving me.

Contents

Acknowledgements	vii
Foreword	xi
Prologue	xv
Introduction	xix

Why bother creating us to live in a broken world?	1
Do we need to be free to experience love?	9
Are struggle and suffering required for virtue?	17
Why not limit our freedom?	23
Are we created in God's image?	29
Does God give us what we ask for?	33
How can God hear everyone's prayers at the same time?	39
How does God answer our prayers	45
How come we can't hear God's voice?	49
Where is God?	55
Why does God remain outside of the world?	59
Is God a psychological projection?	63
Why all the rules and boundaries?	69
If God knows our choices ahead of time, are we free?	73
How does God comfort us?	77
How does God work through others?	81

Why natural evil?	87
How can God love six billion children?	93
Does God care for us more than his other creations?	97
Can Christianity be truer than other religions?	101
Does God care what career we choose?	107
Does God have a specific mission for me?	113
Does God favour the spiritually mature over the spiritual infant?	119
How does God react to our anger?	123
Can God be disappointed with us?	127
Will God send his children to hell?	131
Why does God have to pay our debt?	139
Does heaven exist?	145
Afterword	151

Foreword

IT WAS LATE AFTERNOON ON SEPTEMBER 16, 2012. MY WIFE Karen and I had just travelled over ten thousand kilometres from our home in Amherstburg, Ontario, Canada to Fujian, China. It was here that we found ourselves sitting at a large oak table inside a spacious conference room located in the hotel we were staying at for the next seven days. We were waiting with nervous anticipation for the arrival of our adopted ten-month-old daughter, who we had named Paige.

Thinking back to that day, I couldn't help but reflect on the journey that led us both to this very moment in China. My wife Karen and I had struggled for fifteen years to have a child. We tried just about every medical procedure that was available, from artificial insemination to in vitro fertilization, over the course of the first eight years of our marriage. The frustrating part of it all was that none of the procedures worked. We were left asking the question that many people have asked during their own life struggles: "Why is God allowing this to happen in my life?" We had hopes and dreams of loving a child of our own—that was, of course, our plan. It apparently was not God's plan for us.

I believe this is when God instilled in Karen and me the calling to international adoption. It would take six years before we would find ourselves in that boardroom, waiting for Paige to be placed in our arms and to finally meet her for the first time. In the preceding years, I had felt that God was preparing me to be the father that I needed to be for my precious daughter.

Growing up in an Italian family had its challenges. I was blessed to have a great mother who loved her children with all her heart and worked extremely hard to make sure we were provided for. My father, on the other hand, was not great by any standard. He was self-centred, never really worked very hard, and relied on my mother to do all the heavy lifting when it came to taking care of our family. It seemed that in his mind, he came first and the rest of us didn't matter. I can't remember my father ever saying the words "I love you", but many times, I do remember being on the receiving end of hurtful words. He would call me "fatso" and "stupid." These insults came during my younger years, a time when fathers are to build you up, not tear you down. Those hurtful words struck me down with force, and still do to this very day.

Unlike my younger brother and sister, who were also very much on the receiving end of his insults, I decided to try and build a relationship with my father. I figured as we got older, he would change with age and possibly see his error. Unfortunately, that didn't happen. When I turned thirty-four, my mother had enough of their toxic marriage and filed for divorce. This was a very difficult time for me. I knew that the father I had always imagined was not to be. I wanted a father that loved his children, worked hard to make a good life, and above all, was capable of expressing his love and affection towards us.

FROM ONE FATHER TO ANOTHER

For as long as I can remember, I always looked at the relationships within my circle of friends, between them and their own fathers, and distinctly remember how much I desired what they had—that special bond a father and son typically share. I will forever be grateful to God for blessing me with my loving mother. If not for her I don't know where I would be today, or the type of person I would have turned out to be.

For all that I lacked in the guidance of a good and caring father during my childhood years, God placed special people in my life. I was blessed to have mentors who challenged me to be better and do better in all aspects of my life. I will forever be grateful for the lessons bestowed upon me that taught me how to be a good and loving father.

It is my belief that as parents we should never make our children feel small. They should be made to feel like giants. A mother should say the words "I love you" as many times in the day as she can. A father and mother should encourage their child's imagination and ideas, no matter how outlandish they may be. Parents should place their child on their shoulders from time to time because the view is amazing for them.

When Paige was finally placed in our arms on that momentous day in China, God blessed us with an incredible gift. As our journey finally intersected with Paige's, we realized that the struggle we had endured was truly worth it. A new chapter was now beginning. The lessons from God will never stop, however, as we continue to learn about His love through our precious child.

In the pages that follow, Kevin describes insights he gained through fatherhood about God's loving character, motives, and unrelenting love. The book addresses the big and sometimes troublesome questions most of us face when trying to walk with God. Kevin does this by relating the experiences common to most parents: experiences of hope, joy, struggle, anguish, and love, to God the Father, who, as Scripture assures us, shares these same experiences with us and lives them much more fully than we can ever imagine. God has hopes and dreams for his children as most parents do. God also disciplines his children, allowing certain mistakes in their lives which build character and virtue. He does this to help us grow, gain our trust, and draw us into relationship with him.

I can tell you that my own journey of bringing my daughter home confirms the lengths God will go to in an effort to bring his children home, make them know his love, and never feel like orphans in this mixed world of beauty and strife. Karen and I were determined to seek Paige out and to share our love with her. I can imagine God feels the same about all of us. This book is about getting in touch with your own parental heart in hopes that you will connect more deeply to God's.

—Piero Amicone, Amherstburg, ON
September 2019

Prologue

THIS BOOK FITS INTO THE FIELD OF CHRISTIAN APOLOGETICS. For those not familiar with this term, the word "apologetic" means defence. Even though this book technically falls into that category, I am not going to be arguing for God's existence here. I hope to take up that topic more thoroughly in future writings, although demonstrating to others that there is more than enough evidence to reasonably believe in God's existence is one of my favourite discussions. This book is more about "who" God is in an experiential sense rather than "if" God exists in a more philosophical manner. So if you are looking for a debate on God's existence, I humbly direct you to the many other scholastic apologetic works in print.

That being said, I do wish to say something before moving on to the more personal apologetic I offer in the following pages. I understand and deeply appreciate the ontological, teleological, and cosmological arguments for God's existence. I also appreciate the moral argument for God's existence, as well as various types of evidence provided by biochemistry, neurophysiology, and general philosophy. These arguments and forms of evidence have led me quite deeply to an intellectual belief in God's existence, and I owe much to them for getting me there.

However, believing God exists and knowing God personally are clearly two different things. Psalm 14:1 reads, *"The fool says in his heart, 'There is no God'"* (RSV). I was once a fool. It was a long journey to get to where I am now, and I no longer have a fool's heart. I now have a personal relationship with God. This relationship is not perfect by any means (on my part at least), but it is still an actual relationship.

Just as I am taking God's existence as a given rather than arguing for it, I firmly believe that we have free will and won't be arguing this topic here either. Over the years, I have had many conversations and debates with people who have tried to convince me otherwise. Their arguments seem a little eccentric and not based on real world experience, as well as lacking any convincing evidence or basis in truth. Therefore, I will only briefly point out the logical contradiction of this conclusion to show how our assumed freedom is part and parcel of the functioning of our everyday lives, and will be relevant to what follows in this book.

Take, for instance, a court of law. If we are to argue that none of us are truly free, and that everything is predetermined or determined by a succession of events over which we ultimately have no control, then why should we punish people for something they had no power over choosing in the first place? Think of our justice system. We must assume free will for our courts to be rational, just, and meaningful. The dilemma gets ridiculous if we believe that every event—even the construction of the courts and their guiding laws—came about by an unlawful, unguided, or predetermined succession of events. If that were true, we'd be no more than dominoes in an endless succession awaiting our turn to be acted upon. Our actions would be without any forethought in reason or consequence that was not in some way forced upon us. Within this model, institutions such as the courts, the laws that underpin them, and the consequences of any actions that go against those laws become nothing more than mandatory happenings, deserving of no more punishment than a rock falling from a cliff onto an innocent hiker.

Free will must be assumed to give any meaning to actions that are deserving of punishment as well as for any actions worthy of praise. This is just one of many reasons why I will not be arguing this point in greater detail throughout the book, and I trust that your reason and everyday experience will lead you to the same conclusion, thereby avoiding any barriers to the following insights concerning God's existence and our free will. I believe God exists and that he created us free. As to why God made these choices, I think we can make some reasonable progress.

This book will pose questions regarding God's intentions and motivations, followed by my experiences as a father and my reflections on how those experiences may be similar to God's experiences in relation to us. I'm well aware that my experiences as a father are substantially smaller and less significant than those of God our Heavenly Father, with far less knowledge, insight, and understanding behind them.

At the end of each chapter there are reflection questions I have come up with. I hope that you take the time to ponder them. In fact, questions are the whole basis for this book, and the foundation for the insights that came to me through my experiences as a father. The basis for knowledge and wisdom usually starts with asking questions, and James 1:5 (RSV) reminds us that God is willing to help us with this: *"If any of you lacks wisdom, let him ask God, who gives to all generously and without reproaching...."* If you choose to skip over these questions, you may very well miss out on greater insights that can come directly from the answers you give. I was pleasantly surprised by how God led me to deeper understanding through the process of inquiry, and I believe that this will be the case for you too if you take the opportunity.

I recognize that no metaphor is perfect, especially any metaphor that aims at describing God. Christian philosopher and apologist William Lane Craig points this out in the following quote, "…God is supposed to serve as a model for parenthood. But while there are analogies between God as our Heavenly Father and a human parent, the disanalogies are so great as to undermine the assumption that God is to serve as a role model for human parents."[1] I agree with Craig to some extent, but I don't believe that the insights or understanding obtained through this comparison are significantly undermined; however, we must keep in mind that we are talking about God, who ultimately is not our equal in the way we are to our children. Plenty of personal stories from my own life will be used as examples to back these insights, and hopefully be beneficial in describing what God (the ultimate Father) is trying to tell us about how much he loves us and why we should trust him, and that one day it will all make sense.

---

[1] William Lane Craig, "#302: Why We Raised Our Kids to Believe in God," *Reasonable Faith with William Lane Craig*, January 26, 2013 (https://www.reasonablefaith.org/writings/question-answer/why-we-raised-our-kids-to-believe-in-god/).

Introduction

AT BEDTIME ONE NIGHT, MY SON OWEN ASKED ME A question. In his innocent and curious manner, he half-whispered, "Why did God create us, Dad?" As you can imagine, the answer didn't come easily. Had this question been posed by an adult with a solid base of theological or philosophical backing, a very lively conversation could have ensued. However, Owen is a nine-year-old boy, and I knew such weighty ideas would go over like a lead balloon. Instead, I started by using my own role as a father as an example, hoping to quench some of his curiosity. I told my son that I believe God created us so he could love us, and in turn, hoped we would choose to love him back. I explained that I think God did this freely, just as his mother and I had for him, his sister Kara, and younger brother Luke. I shared with him how his mother and I wished for him to be happy in life, to experience things like making friends, loving others, playing, and helping one another. I watched my son think it over for a few seconds, and I could tell by the smile on his face that this answer satisfied him for now. He turned over and fell asleep, apparently content.

What does this little story have to do with writing about God? Well, to me, fatherhood has everything to do with learning about God. Because for me, there was one more benefit to having children that also caught me by surprise, an obvious one really: for as long as I can remember, I have always referred to God as father, as I'm sure many of you have also. However, I don't honestly know if I used the word as much more than a term of endearment, or as an attempt to throw a sheet over the spirit of the all-powerful God in an attempt to give him some tangible form. I have a father, and I have had a wonderful stepfather in my life for many years before his untimely death, but God is God, not my actual father.

After my daughter Kara was born, I remember starting to understand that God was in fact my father, and not just in the metaphorical sense. The best I can describe how this subtly dawned on me is that it was as if God was speaking to me as one father to another. It seemed God was saying to me, "Do you see what I mean? Do you understand what I feel now? Can you see why I would allow struggle and pain?"

In these opening stages of being a father, I started to understand truths about God that I could never really grasp on my own. Many tough questions now seemed to have credible answers. For example, answers to questions like why God created us in the first place and why he would allow us to live in such a broken world now seemed to make more sense, or why God would allow suffering and free will knowing their immediate and future consequences. These questions are just a few examples of many that had flooded my thoughts that now seemed less arduous to consider.

I know God reveals himself to people in different ways, and here I was feeling that God was revealing himself and truths about our existence and our ultimate purpose in a deeper way than reason alone was able to. God was apparently doing this through my experiences of being a father.

I had felt for so long that answers to questions concerning God's motives and intentions were completely out of limits for our finite minds. It had been like these answers were on the other side of huge locked doors within my mind and would forever remain an unreachable mystery. It now seemed that God was handing me a key to those huge doors and allowing me access. I assume everyone's set of keys are different, but I know that for me, my key to understanding God more fully was fatherhood.

One thing needs to be made clear. I am not saying that my experiences of being a father have imparted upon me everything that could ever be known about God. Yet, it must be said that Jesus used sheep, coins, and wheat to explain God's truths, motives, and intentions to people of his day—so why couldn't God use my own children and my experience of being a father to teach me? As the saying goes, "from one to another"—or in this case, from one father to another.

In fact, Jesus used fatherhood directly to relate God's love and final objectives to people many times. Two passages immediately come to mind. In Mathew 7:11 (RSV) Jesus says, *"If you, then, who are evil, know how to give good gifts to your children, how much more will your Father who is in heaven give good things to those who ask him!"* And in the parable of the prodigal son (Luke 15:11–32), God's love again is described in terms of human fatherhood as the prodigal's father welcomes a broken, sorrowful child back home after a lengthy and disastrous rebellion.

Jesus tells us to call God "Abba" (father). There is good reason for this. I personally think God wants us to know that he loves us individually and intimately—like our own mother or father do, but even more fully and in a more perfect and complete way. Now, I also realize that not everyone has had the good fortune of having loving parents. I know many people that didn't have parents that set a good example of love and protection. Yet they are very mindful that their own parents missed the mark through their own sin, and know intuitively what a good parent should be. My best bet is that even if you've been ill-fated enough to have experienced bad parenting in your life, you will still be moved by God's intention to love you like his very own precious child, especially if you now have your own children.

In what follows, I will share some of what I feel God showed me to be true about himself, and what I know to be true about God (the perfect heavenly father) through my own experiences as Kevin Jarvis (the far from perfect human father).

In the end, I also get a sense that I'm writing this book for me. I'm constantly trying to grow closer to God and grasp his purpose for my life, and for that matter, the purpose of everything under the sun. I believe that through fatherhood, God has given me a glimpse into his very own heart, and I plan on fleshing out these reflections for my own understanding, and hopefully for yours too.

Why bother creating us to live in a broken world?

For I know the plans I have for you, says the Lord,
plans for welfare and not for evil,
to give you a future and a hope.
(Jeremiah 29:11, RSV)

THE WORLD IS IN CRISIS, AND ALWAYS HAS BEEN. WARS, disease, natural disasters, suffering, and the violence of nature itself all beg the question: is this a world a loving God would create for his beloved? If God knew ahead of time that things would be this grueling, then are we not naturally inclined to ask, "Why bother anyway?" I think the question has visited most of us at one time or another. For some, myself included, the question ceases to be a mere visitor and takes up full-time residence in our minds. For many years, my mind was plagued with questions like these.

I used to rationalize that God's motives are not to be known, destined to remain a mystery that forever eludes our finite minds. Acceptance of scripture and a bolstered faith were the only way to move forward with any peace of mind, but this reasoning never completely satisfied me. I think dissatisfaction with trite answers is built into our reasoning minds, as my four-year-old son reminded me one winter afternoon.

It was a particularly cold, windy winter day when my son asked if he could go outside to play for a while. Like most parents during a non-school day, I was very busy and so rather briskly answered my son, "No, not right now." He clearly wasn't satisfied with my answer and asked several more times within the hour. Over the years, I have learned that giving any one of my kids a simple answer without a reason leads inevitably to even more questions. The next question he asked was an obvious one that I'm sure you can see coming. It is humble, and yes, at times annoying; nevertheless, in the end it is justified.

After each time I answered my son "No," he would ask, "Why?"

I soon realized that my son was not so much challenging me to change my decision to go outside as he was demanding an explanation. I decided to take the time with my son instead of brushing him off in haste. Looking into his eyes as I went down on one knee, I calmly explained to him that the temperature outside was way too cold and that it would be rather dangerous to be outside right now. I then proceeded to bring my son to the window, show him the blowing snow, and point out that there were no other children outside. After a moment, and with that familiar four-year-old drawl, my son muttered, "Okay," as he hung his head and made his way back downstairs. Halfway down the stairs I heard my son call up, now with a more excited pitch, "Daddy, can we have a Pokémon battle then?" I knew I had good reason to deny playtime outside, but to deny a

Pokémon battle when nothing was really pressing would be unreasonable.

I remember many occasions when my wife and I discussed starting a family and why we wanted children. Even early on, we were both quite certain having children was in our plans, but inquiring *why* we wanted children sparked some great discussions. We talked about wanting to see our children grow and develop as unique individuals. The idea of being able to contribute in a very distinct way to their character, attitude, and growth was an awesome thought to both of us. Obviously, the notion of experiencing this special kind of love for a child, and receiving a special measure back, was an endearing motivation, as well as a frightening responsibility.

Many dark possibilities often entered the conversation as well. For instance, we questioned the state of the world and the many challenges that we would face in raising children in such a chaotic and seemingly callous environment. We knew that any children we brought into this world would not live without some degree of pain, disillusionment, and despair. There were the guaranteed heartbreaks: their loss of innocence and the tragedies that would befall them and eventually everyone around them, including death. We found ourselves questioning if we would really want to bring children into a world where anxiety, fear and despair would at times be their perennial experience. Ultimately, our decision came down to two questions: would it be worth it, and would it be meaningful?

My wife and I truly believe that having children has been worth it. Although the sinister, cruel motives of individuals, nations, and even their own selves will bring about much anguish in their lives, I know that love, peace, friendship, beauty, freedom, virtue, passion, self-expression, contemplation, and numerous other graces will touch them in deep and profound ways as well. We both feel that such graces could (and hopefully will) eventually move them towards inner peace, understanding, and appreciation for all this life has to offer.

This is how I suspect God felt when he first thought of creating a world with us in mind. Maybe, like my wife and I once had, God measured the rewards as being worth the cost. As I look back on my days as a single person, I consider that I could have lived my entire life without children and probably still experienced a fair share of the satisfaction I longed for— probably more if looking at it from a self-serving standpoint. However, I freely chose to share my love by having children, hoping that I would feel some of that love returned to me. It was not a rash decision by any means.

Surely God didn't need us to be content, and certainly he didn't create us because he was lonely—yet at some point I think God decided he wanted more than mere carnal creations such as dinosaurs and fish that obeyed only by instinct and physical law in his created universe. As funny as this may sound, I believe God chose to have children. And I also believe that God considered some of the same issues my wife and I explored, although in an infinitely more insightful way. God knew we were going to go wrong sometimes and hurt ourselves and others. He also recognized that there would be heartache, death, and loss to deal with. I'm pretty sure God foresaw the many consequences—good and bad—of creating beings that were free to act in accordance with their own will, just as my wife and I could anticipate the very same possibilities for our own children. God understood that there could be real evil and much anguish as a result.

I think we would be remiss to suppose that God didn't reflect on, foresee, and distress over the possible outcomes for all of us. Again, my wife and I considered these very same things before having our own children. We thought of the many potentially horrendous life scenarios for our children. We were very certain that our children would hurt, most assuredly suffer, and eventually experience the ultimate betrayal of life—death. Is there not a parent that hasn't experienced these haunting anxieties before the arrival of their child?

So why does God allow us to live in such a hurting world if he loves us so much? I've always sensed the same dilemma; however, I can quickly turn the tables on myself. I can ask myself the same question.

One afternoon, after learning of a friends terminal diagnosis, I was taking a walk and was begging God to help me understand why he bothered creating us to live in such a broken world. I wanted to know why he allowed us to experience a life so full of struggle and pain, where we have to confront so much loss and death. At that moment I understood that if I was to ask God for an answer to this question, then I would first have to answer it myself. If I am willing to curse God for bringing me into a broken and hurting world so full of sorrow, then shouldn't I also openly question my own motives for doing the very same thing regarding my own three children? Shouldn't we all? If we are willing to ask God why he would choose to create us to live in a broken world so full of pain and suffering, then must we not also ask ourselves why we choose to do the very same thing by having kids of our own? Could the benefits perhaps outweigh the pitfalls despite these ugly facts? Can we charge God as unloving for this supposed crime, and at the same time exclude our own intentions?

Knowing how extremely limited I am in knowledge, wisdom, and the intricate workings of God's universe, how is it that I still concluded it was a worthy act to have children and that it would be beneficial for them to experience this troubled world, all the while looking beyond the dark curtain of evil and suffering it contains? Can I not see that God in his unlimited knowledge and wisdom, far beyond the limits of human reasoning and understanding, would also see it fit that my soul would benefit from this brief embodiment? I would also wager that most parents given to thinking about this question would also agree that the many pitfalls and struggles of a life lived on this planet are in the end won out by the potential blessings. If you can get this far, then I think it's not too extreme of a leap to perhaps look at God's reasons for putting us on this broken planet as ultimately meaningful—and yes, even truly worth it.

My hope is that one day my children will look to me, their own human father, and make this same connection between my choice and God's. Perhaps they will intuitively sense that if their own parents thought it worth the cost to bring them into this world despite its failings, then maybe God, the Father of us all, believed the same for us, too. Perhaps if I do a better than "just good enough" job of loving them, they'll realize that the imperfect, crippled, and human love they receive from me is nothing in comparison to the more perfect and awesome love of God.

QUESTIONS TO PONDER

1. Do you find yourself questioning God's motives for creating us to live in such a world as this?

2. If you are a parent and brought a child into this world, how would you answer your child if they asked you what your motives were when deciding to have them?

3. Take a moment to reflect on these motives for having children. If you are not a parent, what do you think your parents' motives were to have you?

4. Can you see how God may have had some of the same motivations?

Do we need to be free to experience love?

If the beloved is transformed into an automaton, the lover finds himself alone.
—Jean-Paul Sartre[2]

IF WE CAN UNDERSTAND WHY IT MIGHT MAKE SENSE THAT God created us and decided to bring us into this world based on our very own motives for doing the same for our children, then I think it is evident why he would want those creations to be truly free. He would want this for the same reasons I want my children to be free in choice and consequence. I want my children to truly and freely love me. I don't want their love to be predetermined or made obligatory, and I also want them to become morally sound persons, free to develop strong virtues such as courage, faith, and compassion. I'm sure you want some of the same things for your children. Nevertheless, I am aware that most of us take for granted how these objectives come about at all. Our freedom of choice is what makes this

---

[2] Quoted at "If God is a Loving God, Why Does He Allow Suffering?," *Pastor Brad Abley's Blog*, March 23, 2016 (https://pastorbradabley.wordpress.com/2016/03/23/if-god-is-a-loving-god-why-does-he-allow-suffering/).

possible; it not only enables love, but all the virtues most of us aspire to as well. For instance, do you believe that you could become a compassionate person without the ability to turn a blind eye to suffering? Or do you foresee yourself mounting any amount of courage in the absence of dreadful or frightening situations? How about developing an honest character without the capability of deception? If God wanted children truly created in his image while maintaining the potential for them to experience authentic love or to develop real virtue, he would have had to make them free, wouldn't he?

You may wonder, as I have many times, why God didn't just create us to be virtuous in the first place and avoid all the trouble; however, answer the following honestly: do you find a person who books a helicopter to the top of a mountain more adventurous, brave, and accomplished than a person who climbs it himself? I cannot imagine forgoing all the little milestones in my children's lives like the first time they showed real compassion to another person, the first sign of independence or bravery as they chose to sleep alone in their bedroom or take their own shower. As small as these things are, I recognize them as the building blocks to conquering greater fears, acting more compassionately, and having the confidence and courage to go it alone in the future.

I'm getting ahead of myself here. I will talk more about freedom and the possibility of suffering being necessary for growth and virtue in the following chapter, but for now let's go back to the original question of freedom being required for real love to flourish.

The nighttime routine around our house mirrors that of many other families. We help our children to settle down for the evening by allowing them to pick out some books to read, decide which pajamas to wear, and choose a healthy snack. After this, we tuck them in for the night. The best part of this routine is when I get a tiny hug and a voluntary, "I *lub* you," from my daughter, or a sincere, "You're the best daddy ever," from one of my boys as they hug me with surprising strength for such little guys. It isn't every night that one of these special moments happens. Sometimes my wife or I receive these tender utterances from their lips, and that's what makes them special and meaningful. There have been many nights when I can barely hide the subtle welling of tears in my eyes as these words are whispered by one of my children. In these moments, the day's trials, little battles and tantrums all are forgotten, and what remains is the bursting emotion of love, fulfillment, and gratitude. If you can remember similar experiences then I'm sure you could also imagine how unmoving these words and gestures would be if they were offered as programmed or predetermined responses.

A few weeks ago, we attended a large dinner gathering for my sister in law's birthday. As we were eating dinner, I noticed that my son wasn't eating his meal. In my infinite fatherly wisdom, I decided I would play a game with him. I told my son that my cell phone was a remote control and he was a robot and that when I pushed a button and said a command, he had to follow the order. Thankfully hoodwinked, my son agreed to play along. I started by issuing little commands: "Robot roll up sleeves, Robot sit straight in the chair." My son answered the commands in his best staccato robot voice, "Ye us da dee." I eventually got around to giving commands like "Eat chicken" and "Take small French fry." By this time, my son was already fully on board with the game, and much to his amusement, the other adults at the table were playing along as well, telling him that he was such a good robot and issuing small commands themselves. After most of his dinner was successfully devoured, he wanted to keep playing. I commanded him to go hug his grandmother across the table, then to hug his aunt who was sitting beside her. My son briskly followed the commands. The last command I issued was to go give his papa, who was sitting across the room at a different table, a big hug. He continued to play along for a bit, but eventually lost his enthusiasm to oblige commands and drifted off to play by himself. I recall my wife's Aunt Jill commenting half-jokingly, "That would sure make things easier, now wouldn't it." Everyone let out an agreeable laugh, me included. But two things stood out for me while playing this little game. The first thing I noticed was that when my son hugged his grandmother and aunt, who were sitting with us at our table, they humoured him by barely tightening their grip as they gave him what I would call the "acquaintance hug," laughing and half-heartedly thanking my son with contrived verbiage like "Ah, thanks buddy." The second thing I noticed was that when my son made his way across the room to hug his papa (who wasn't aware of the game going on, as it was a thirty person dinner with three tables) and jumped onto his lap, the ten or so people around him at his table responded with "Ah, that's so precious," as my father-in-law held his grandson like he was receiving the best gift ever given. His papa was not aware that my son had been commanded to hug him, and was merely playing along with a game.

I think it's worthwhile to take the two reactions seriously and consider if they offer any insight into how we feel about freely given love as compared to obligatory, programmed actions that appear loving. I think most parents would agree that if the only reason we ever received affection from our children was because it was impossible for them to do otherwise, we would feel cheated. Our children's love for us would be a fraudulent transaction. Is it not true that for love to exist, there needs to be a choice involved? I'm certain this is the case, and I am equally confident that God saw this dilemma as well and quite assuredly came to the same conclusion as you and I would. Love demanded is not love received, like paying with real money and receiving only counterfeit bills for change. For God to truly receive love from his children, he would have no other choice but to make them just as free to not love him.

The thought often strikes me that one day, as in the parable of the prodigal son in the New Testament, one of my sons or my daughter could in fact turn their hearts from my love. They could leave and demand that I stay away. They could reject my love for them and refuse to act on their love for me. To date I have not had this experience, but I do know friends with older children who are in this predicament as I write this. Is it hurtful? According to them, extremely so. These very same people say that they would not go back and forgo the love, affection, and pride of watching their children come into their own that they had the privilege of experiencing in days past, despite their child's current state of rebellion or distance. The struggle once again seems to be judged as worth the possible consequences.

How many times have I barely given God a moment of my attention, or said a half-hearted prayer more out of obligation rather than real passion? Plenty, to be sure. I also know of many people, friends included, who have made the choice to not even acknowledge God or his love in their lives in any way at all.

> *"My people have committed two sins: they have forsaken me, the spring of living water, and have dug out their own cisterns, broken cisterns that cannot hold water."* (Jeremiah 2:13, NIV)

With these consequences and more in mind, God still apparently considered these possibilities as worth the risk.

Ultimately, God could have chosen not to create us in the first place, therefore eliminating the risk of his love being rejected. Thankfully, this is not the case.

QUESTIONS TO PONDER

1. Can you see the difference that love offered freely and love demanded would make in your relationships, especially with your children?

2. Can you think of a time a free expression of love or appreciation from one of your children melted your heart? Can you see that God may feel the same about you?

3. Reflect on the potential for your children to one day reject your love or rebel against your good will for them. How does this make you feel?

4. Reflect on that fact that you knew this potential existed before bringing your children into the world, and that their free will could bring about disastrous consequences for you and for them. Why did you choose to have children despite these risks?

5. Reflect on the hopes and plans you have for your children's happiness and how it would make you feel if they turned from you, forging their own destructive path. How does this make you feel?

Are struggle and suffering required for virtue?

If there's a power above us (and that there is all nature cries aloud through all her works), he must delight in virtue.
—Joseph Addison[3]

I BELIEVE IT'S IMPORTANT TO CONSIDER THAT GOD'S CHOICE to grant us freedom so we can give and receive meaningful love also makes all the virtues we hold possible as well. Take a minute to imagine developing any virtue without the free will that we take for granted. The struggles we face allow the forging of these virtues, eventually building them into permanent parts of our character. If we didn't have the option to ignore suffering, cower in the face of fear, give up on worthy goals, take a stand against injustice, or choose to give time to those in need, would we truly be able to develop virtue in any meaningful way? C.S. Lewis makes this point in his book *The Problem of Pain* when he says, "try to exclude the possibility of suffering which the

---

[3] Quoted at https://quotes.yourdictionary.com/author/joseph-addison/142489.

order of nature and the existence of free will involves, and you find that you have excluded life itself."[4]

Would our children be robbed of opportunities for growth if they were denied their free will and the consequences of their actions? They would. When my wife and I imagined having children, it went without saying that we would be relying largely on our children's power of choice as well as their capability of working against their own dispositions, which most of the time would lead them down a path towards fear, selfishness, despair, anger, lust, evil, and ultimately suffering. Instead, we both hoped and anticipated that our children would struggle down the virtuous path that leads to qualities more resembling peace, sacrifice, hope, compassion, love, and goodness, and most of us know that fighting against our darker dispositions is often a continuous struggle and the more difficult route.

Jesus once said that the path that leads to life (virtue, righteousness) is narrow, and few take it (Matthew 7:14). I will do anything within my power to help my own children enter through the narrow gate, and I hardly believe the entrance will be crowded.

Life can be unfair and painful, and truthfully some days I do wish God would take away our free will and all the suffering that comes along with it. I'm sure there will be many days when I will wish to take away my children's struggles and suffering, but at what expense would that come? I would love to live in a world without murderers and rapists, but I also know that a world without such people would also have to be a world without heroes and saints. It would seem that some level of struggle and suffering is what actually forges virtue in our souls. Again, I

---

[4] Armand Nicholi, *The Question of God: C.S. Lewis and Sigmund Freud Debate God, Love, Sex, and the Meaning of Life* (New York, NY: Simon & Schuster, 2003), p. 211.

turn to C.S. Lewis, who writes, "If the world is indeed a 'vale of soul making' it seems on the whole to be doing its work."[5] The consequences of rejection, rebellion, and even evil are part of the risk. Again, we ourselves as parents willingly take this same risk, so why wouldn't God take on that same risk in hopes of reaping the reward of seeing his children develop real virtue?

It would appear in the end that God is more concerned with our holiness than our happiness, and what's best for us rather than what makes us the most pleased. We all know of parents who remove every obstacle and provide anything their children's little hearts desire, and we also know what kind of adults that parenting model creates. I can't count how many times my kids have asked for ice cream or cookies for dinner, only to find meat, carrots and mashed potatoes on their plates. Just like any loving parent would, we find that God more often gives us what we need than what we want.

All this is not to say that we like suffering and struggle, or that we desire it for our children. By way of illustration, as a minor hockey coach for my son's team for the past several seasons, I have realized in a very real way that you don't get hockey players by just lacing up their skates and throwing them on the ice with a stick in their hands. Obstacles, challenges, drills, coaching, repetition, and fun are how you make hockey players. It would be a lot easier for the coach if all kids possessed innate hockey skills when they stepped on the ice—this would surely eliminate most, if not all, of the frustration, effort, and challenge coaches face. But I know it would also eliminate the joys of seeing a player into whom I put effort and instruction

---

[5] C.S. Lewis, *The Problem of Pain* (London: Geoffrey Bles & the Centenary Press, 1946), p. 96.

finally skate down the ice on their own or score their first goal. As a parent and coach, what made seeing my son skate down the ice and score his first goal so special was the contrast between where he started out (he couldn't stand on his skates for the first three practices) and where he is now as a legitimate hockey player. Even more awesome than the pride I feel for him is seeing the pride he feels in himself, and the smile on his face. After that goal, he knew he had achieved something, and I can't imagine taking that away from him.

As parents, we see that our kids sometimes get mad at us and feel distressed when they don't understand our intentions for them. For example, my son probably thought I was being a horrible dad when I let him fall on the ice several times after letting go of him while teaching him to skate, or perhaps my daughter or my youngest son may have thought that I was being unfair and neglectful by making them clean their own room or walk to their friend's house all by themselves. There are so many times our kids can perceive our actions as unfair, unloving, or downright cruel. However, we know that there is a higher objective behind these decisions. Just because a four-year-old may not understand why their parents make them go through certain experiences or demand certain tasks to be completed, it doesn't follow that there isn't a good reason at all. The gap of knowledge and foresight between our children and us causes this to often be the case.

Considering, then, the gap of knowledge between us and God, couldn't there be a reason we might not grasp behind God's intentions and objectives (based as they are upon infinite knowledge) in creating a world where pain, distress, and struggle are allowed, and purposely employed to build virtue? My son slowly came to trust that everything I was doing on the ice with him (despite how hard it seemed at the time) was to ultimately make him a better hockey player. The only reason I could stand to watch my son struggle as he cried alone on the ice those first few practices was because I could foresee the result. I saw where he was most likely to end up, and he couldn't. I knew there was an end to the struggle, and I knew the discomfort he was experiencing was not in vain. Maybe, then, God also sees a world where we struggle, sometimes suffer, and work hard to attain virtues and build character as ultimately worth it. I believe that God can see a future saint like I can see a future hockey player, and God, being the ultimate coach, will push us to our limits and cheer us on until we become just that.

We all scream and pound our fists at God for allowing us to experience pain, suffering, and struggle, only to then demand our own children go through various struggles in this life, insisting on the qualities these difficulties will bring to fruition in them. In my forty years on this earth, I have already experienced a fair amount of pain, loss, and fear. I also know that if I was to be completely honest, I would have to say that the only way I have experienced any amount of real growth in my character, or developed any real compassion, insight, or courage, has been through dark and troubling times. I know that my children also must face fear to be courageous, experience suffering to develop compassion, sense hatred to understand true love, and overcome obstacles to grow strong. In the end, if I can look back on my life and be grateful that my parents brought me into this world with all of its ups and downs, sufferings and joys—and even despite my eventual demise—then I could be just as grateful towards God, and perhaps my own children could be just as grateful towards me, and God.

QUESTIONS TO PONDER

1. Can you think of times when obstacles prepared you for a situation in life, whether a relationship, a career, or the ability to serve others?

2. Reflect on some of the obstacles, restrictions, or challenges you place in front of your children. What reasons and end goals do you have in mind?

3. Can you remember a time when your child could not see the good intention behind your actions or deliberately placed obstacles?

4. What virtue can you say you developed through struggle in your own life?

Why not limit our freedom?

There is never a better measure of what a person is than what he does when he's absolutely free to choose.
—William M. Bulger[6]

WHY COULDN'T GOD HAVE CREATED US FREE TO LOVE, and allowed just enough struggle to forge virtues, with just the right amount of pain and suffering to get the job done? Couldn't he have stopped short of total disaster in our lives by preventing us from taking our free will too far—for example, by stopping us from taking actions or making decisions that would harm or even kill others? This question has crossed my mind many times.

One day my son Luke was playing in our front yard with a friend. Suddenly, he picked up a stick from the ground and attempted to hit his friend with it. As you can imagine, I quickly intervened and stopped him. Technically, I momentarily took

---

[6] Steve May, *The Story File: 1001 Contemporary Illustrations for Speakers, Writers and Preachers* (Peabody, MA: Hendrickson Publishers, 2000), p. 38.

away my son's free will, which ultimately prevented injury to his friend, as well as saving my son from facing the consequences of his actions. If we carry this scenario to a more serious situation and replace the stick my son was holding with a knife, a gun, or any other means to inflict injury or death on another person, then the obvious question is "Couldn't God do the same?" I allow my children a certain level of free will, but limit it when it comes to certain actions. If God limited our free will more consistently, would the world not be a much safer place for everyone?

This seems like an impenetrable problem at first glance. On any given day, at least one of my three children does something where I must intervene, and If I didn't, it would probably result in injury to themselves or others. For example, one day I heard a gasp and saw my wife run towards my son Luke's car seat because my daughter was attempting to pick him up by his head. I ran over and grabbed little Luke before his untimely demise could ensue. The same day, my oldest son and daughter got into a pushing match on a bed in one of their rooms after a friendly hide and seek game went sideways. I again intervened. I have prevented my kids from pushing each other down the stairs, walking into the road, hitting one another with various objects, climbing too high, or sticking things up their noses or down their throats. I think you can see the point.

In none of these incidents did I take away my child's free will indefinitely, although I did interfere momentarily to prevent catastrophes and steer their hurtful or mistaken actions in the right direction. If I can do this (making my children and others around them safer), then why can't God do the same?

Why can't God allow our overall free will but still interfere momentarily when the need arises? I have given this much thought, and have come to a few conclusions. Firstly, we must understand that the consequences of allowing or not allowing our children's moral actions as human parents can differ from the discretion, consequence, and goals of God. I once heard a metaphor about caterpillars that explained how the moral responsibilities can differ between human parents and God. What a caterpillar may envision (if they envision anything at all) as the end of their existence is in fact the beginning of new life as a butterfly. If we imagine ourselves as parents of caterpillars, then as caterpillar parents we are concerned with everything about our little caterpillars' existence before the cocoon, while God is concerned with our existence as both caterpillars and butterflies. As caterpillars, we would likely live with the uncertainty of what (if anything) comes of us after the cocoon (grave). If, though, we knew with certainty like God does that death was not the end of our existence but was really a great transition, then we could see how God could go so far as to not eliminate the actions of a murderer, rapist, or thief, since he would also have to forgo the potential of the highest moral valour, virtue, and love.

Can we not see that we allow a certain level of moral freedom in our children's lives just as God does? We often risk consequences that may even lead to death in our children's lives, as is the case when we allow them to drive the family car, hoping they choose not to drink and drive. There is the possibility of moral jeopardy when we allow them to spend time alone with members of the opposite sex, trusting that they will respect boundaries. These are just two examples of the many risks we take in the governing of our children's lives. We give stern warnings and advice to our sons and daughters that will hopefully steer them in the right direction and avoid drastic consequences. We tell them not to smoke, not to drink too much or do drugs. With luck, in any given moral dilemma they face, they will hear our voice in their head and recall our teaching and warnings. Doesn't God do the same through our conscience? God is trying to prevent murder, mass shootings and rape all the time. But just as our children can ignore our warnings and promptings, we can do the same for God's quiet—yet stern—voice in our conscience. When our children make the wrong choice, whether it leads to personal or mortal consequences for themselves or others, ultimately we sanctioned and believed in their moral character to do the right thing when acting alone.

How many times have we watched an interview with the parents of a mass shooter who were utterly shocked and horrified at their child's choices and behaviour? I guess if that parent had been beside that child every moment of every day, then the tragedy could have been prevented. Essentially, for parents to prevent their children from doing anything harmful to themselves or others, they would literally have to be attached at the hip, largely eliminating their free will. That's not practical or desirable, is it?

Is it not possible that God guides us and tries to stop us from making wrong decisions or taking wrong action through the pangs of our conscience, just like we as parents do through our own warnings and exhortations? We must trust that when left to themselves, our children will make wise decisions and act justly. Does God not have to trust us just the same? The difference is that we are concerned with our children's lives before the cocoon, while God is also concerned with our life as butterflies.

QUESTIONS TO PONDER

1. Reflect on the many ways you allow your children moral autonomy and what the potential positive and negative consequences could be.

2. Do you think you could prevent every wrong decision or wrong action in your children's lives?

3. Do you feel God intervenes though conscience, and if so, is it enough of an intervention?

4. Describe how you would have God handle things differently. Would this change the outcome of developing true moral responsibility and virtue?

Are we created in God's image?

So God created man in his own image,
in the image of God he created him;
male and female he created them.
(Genesis 1:27, RSV)

WHEN I CONSIDER IF AND HOW WE ARE CREATED IN GOD'S image, I'm not talking in some anthropomorphic way—as if we possess our physical characteristics because God fashioned us after his own two hands, two feet, and bipedal motion. In that case, God would be the proverbial grey-bearded sage in the sky. I don't think many people believe this to be the case; at least I hope not. With that being said, just as I desire to pass down and instill certain qualities and characteristics I possess to my own children, I believe God made it clear in the Bible that he had the same intention. God cannot create us in his physical image first and foremost because God is not physical (God is spirit: John 4:24.) God's choice to create us in his image has more to do with who God is personally and morally rather than what God is in essence.

We were created in God's image in relation to who he is and what attributes of his character he wants us to possess and participate in. My children will learn more about who they are by looking within themselves rather than in a mirror, and we, too, can look within to discover a little more about who God is because some of his attributes are reflected in us.

I want my children to have some of the curiosity I possess about the world, as well as a sense of moral responsibility. I hope they will be creatively inspired (in whatever form that may take), possess a sense of humour, and be compassionate. These are just a few of the many things I hope to pass on and instill within my children, and although they will never be carbon copies of me (nor would they ever desire to be), they will possess some similarities, both by sharing in my being and from what I teach them through my words and actions. In this sense, my children will dimly reflect an image of me. I can think of many times that people have seen me out with one of my children and commented that they look just like me or my wife. I usually quip jokingly that I hope they look more like my wife. But the comments I appreciate even more are when someone speaks about how creative, well-mannered, or thoughtful they are. These remarks refer to their character, in which I take more pride as a father than I do their physical characteristics.

I'm sure that God wants us to reflect characteristics of his being also. God is love, justice, goodness, and the ultimate artist, and we as his children share and participate in some of these attributes by bestowal. Within myself, I find the desire to end suffering, form friendships, love deeply, and seek justice and goodness, to name just a few. I'm confident that these qualities within me originate from the ultimate source of these qualities; God. Galatians 5:22–23 (NIV) says, *"But the fruit of the Spirit is love, joy, peace, forbearance, kindness, goodness, faithfulness, gentleness and self-control. Against such things there is no law."*

Just as my children can manifest characteristics of mine and share attributes that I possess without fully being me, we also emulate and reflect qualities and attributes of God without being God. Within ourselves we find a sense of morality, the capacity for compassion, love, and forgiveness, and a hatred towards suffering, injustice and death. And, if it is true that we are created in God's image and likeness, then he too must be moral, compassionate, and forgiving, and hate injustice and death. This makes it certain, to me at least, that God is the source of these desires and attributes I find within me. Can you see how this may be true for you as well?

QUESTIONS TO PONDER

1. In what ways do you feel that we are created in God's image?

2. What characteristics or virtues do you hope that your children will share with you? Are physical or character traits more important to you?

3. What attributes and characteristics do you feel that God hopes we share in?

4. Does God love justice? Does God want goodness for all? Is God creative? Does God hate death? Do some of these things ring true within your own soul also?

5. What are some traits you feel you possess that have their origin in God?

Does God give us what we ask for?

Above all else know this: Be prepared at all times for the gifts of God and be ready always for new ones. For God is a thousand times more ready to give than we are to receive.
—Meister Eckhart[7]

IT WAS APPROXIMATELY TWO WEEKS AFTER CHRISTMAS 2017. I was downstairs reading a book when my son Owen sauntered up to me and fell into my lap, letting out a long sigh. I put down my book and asked what was the matter. He rolled over rather dramatically, telling me that he was bored. A few feet away, my daughter echoed his sentiments, much to my surprise. I looked at them both and asked them if we hadn't recently had a Christmas morning where they received many of the most desired items on their Christmas lists. They both agreed that they had, but that they were bored nonetheless. My son proceeded to tell me that there was a cool video game

---

[7] Earnest Claiborn, *Faith = Success: Go Ahead, Walk on Water* (Dallas, TX: St. Paul Press, 2011), p. 164.

that his friend had received for Christmas that he wished he'd asked for. My daughter now wished she'd asked for a hoverboard rather than a karaoke machine. My youngest son was off playing with a plastic coat hanger he hadn't let out of his sight for the last two weeks.

I was struck by how quick the novelty of these things wore off for them. I reminded them of how badly they'd wanted the very things that now failed to grab their interest, but they were not swayed. Switching gears, I asked them if they wanted to wrestle with me. They both jumped all over me before I could prepare for battle. My youngest son joined in and we had an all-out battle royale. We laughed a lot and changed the rules every other second to put them at an advantage.

After a little while, I decided we should go outside for a little hike. My youngest son and daughter were on board; however, my oldest decided against it and was soon again complaining to my wife about how bored he was. I'd really wanted my oldest son to join us and knew that if he'd decided to come along, he would have had a good time, as was always the case. I do sympathize with my son's boredom here, though, because I have felt it many times myself.

When I was in my twenties, I remember praying to God one afternoon for a better job and to meet a girl I could spend my life with. At that time in my life, I was working as a private investigator, and wasn't too thrilled at the prospect of continuing in sleuth work for much longer. I also had some failed longer-term relationships and was starting to think that I'd lost any chance of meeting someone special. This, however, was not to be the case. Within a few months, I met that special someone—now my wife—and landed a job in law enforcement that I had been chasing for two years. I was ecstatic that I'd gotten what I'd asked for; nevertheless, within a few short months I was like my children, complaining only weeks after Christmas of being bored. Suddenly, the job and the girl weren't enough; that is, they weren't enough without the house, car, and children I decided would complete the picture.

Fast forward a few more years. The house, the car, and children, although all blessings in themselves, also failed to bring the peace, happiness, and sense of resolution I so desired. I just kept searching and acquiring new experiences and the material possessions I thought were missing. I felt restless. Maybe some of you have experienced this emptiness and restlessness as well. I once heard this scenario described as the moving goalpost, or the "I'll be happy when…" syndrome.

I had virtually everything I could hope to have in my life, and yet I still felt a yearning for something else, something *more*. Through my own effort and God's guidance I seemed to have most of what I desired, and yet I was standing before him, basically saying that it wasn't enough and I was unsatisfied and bored. The thought that there were other things he could give me that would bring me peace plagued me daily. Boredom was once described to me as the desire to have desires, a thought that still speaks to me today. Everything seems to be subject to the novelty effect, losing its allure after a relatively short period. Once this takes effect, we often then search elsewhere for something else that won't lose its sheen, like trying to preserve the new car smell for as long as possible. The desires we pine after are relentless to the soul, just as mosquitos are to the body. The unrelenting search for peace is like spooning the last remnants of ice cream from the bowl. The less ice cream there is, the more fervent the effort becomes, with less and less satisfaction.

When my children approached me with their boredom, I responded with my presence, and I believe God does the same. I realized that nothing my children were asking for would relieve their boredom for good, and I'm positive God knows this is true for us as well. I got down on the floor and spent time with my children. It didn't matter whether we wrestled or played with their toys; what mattered was that we spent time together.

Perhaps God also gets down on the floor with us and offers us his presence. Just as my children chose whether or not they would spend time with me, we also make that choice every day. We can turn back to the various material things, our addictions or new and different experiences in our life for our peace and happiness, or we can accept God's invitation for a great adventure with him. We can choose to be in his presence and build relationship, or go off in search for something *more*.

Quite likely, if our desires were in proper order, boredom would not haunt us so relentlessly. Perhaps our focus is on what we get from God rather than his presence. God offers his presence as a father looking to spend time with his children. It would make a huge difference if we could see that something *more* apart from God does not in fact exist. I don't think it has ever been said better that Augustine when he professed, "You have made us for yourself, O Lord, and our heart is restless until it finds rest in you."[8] I hope to rest in peace long before

---

[8] St. Augustine of Hippo, *The Confessions of St. Augustine, Vol. 1* (Griffin, Farran, Browne, 1886), p. 1.

"R.I.P." appears on my tombstone, and I know, as Augustine does, that this peace comes from God, not the world: *"Peace I leave with you; my peace I give you. I do not give to you as the world gives"* (John 14:27, NIV).

QUESTIONS TO PONDER

1. Think of the last time you were bored. Can you identify what you thought was missing that would fix the problem? Did it?

2. Do you feel God's presence in your life? Why or why not?

3. Is God's presence enough for you or do you still feel like something is missing?

4. Does the moving goalpost or the "I'll be happy when…" syndrome ring a bell for you?

5. Do you feel that spending time with God could fulfill your desires? Why or why not?

How can God hear everyone's prayers at the same time?

*Then you will call on me and come
and pray to me, and I will listen to you.*
(Jeremiah 29:12, NIV)

"HOW CAN GOD HEAR ALL OF OUR PRAYERS AT THE SAME time, Daddy?" asked my daughter Kara one night while I was tucking her in. The number of times I have struggled with this question myself approaches the infinite. With this in mind, I suppose the answer to this question is a matter of comparing finite capability to infinite capabilities.

That night I told my daughter a story about a morning around our house. It was during breakfast. My three children and one of my son's friends were all waking up and wandering into the kitchen. My daughter wanted cookies for breakfast, my oldest son wanted to know where his tablet was, I was aware that my youngest son needed a diaper change, and my oldest son's friend was wondering what time his mom was supposed to be coming to take him home. Within a very brief moment, I heard and understood all of their particular needs and requests, as well as becoming aware of their unvoiced needs (my son's need for a diaper change, my daughter's need to use the washroom), and within a very short time frame, I was able to deny my daughter cookies, send her to the washroom, and tell her to pour some cereal for herself. I then informed my oldest son that his tablet was off limits until later. Next I sent a text to the mother of my son's friend, asking what time she was picking him up, and then promptly carried my youngest son for his diaper change. I felt I did a pretty good job.

The parallel speaks for itself. If God is an infinite being, couldn't he hear many prayers, answer or deny requests, and meet the unvoiced needs of his numerous children within brief amounts of time also? If I can do this with four children—and quite possibly a few more, as teachers and coaches do—then is it that far of a stretch to see how God might be able to do the same, considering his infinite nature?

It must also be noted that as finite beings we experience time far differently than God does. A quick example will illustrate this. Before travelling to our trailer in Bayfield, Ontario (which is approximately three hours from our home), my wife and I plan things like washroom breaks, snacks that each of our children prefer, and entertainment. We gather a bag of clothes and some of our kids' toys and books, strap on their safety belts, and start on our way. Many times, before our kids can even say they are bored or hungry, my wife is already doling out various items for these unvoiced requests. We will pull into the service station just as our youngest son needs a diaper change, and get lunch right before the longest stretch of travel so the kids can nap and not get too restless.

Our children take it for granted that we have prepared for their sustenance, contentment, and safety well beforehand, but we have nonetheless. Couldn't God have already prepared and planned for our travels also? Just as my wife and I can foresee the needs and requests of our children well before they are voiced, can't God do the same for us? A prayer that we are uttering in the moment could have already been dealt with by God a long time before that moment came to pass. Maybe God anticipates what we need on our life journeys and knows when and how to bring about these things in large ways, just as my wife and I can do in smaller ways for our own children.

I love how my GPS reroutes me if I make a wrong turn or fail to follow the suggested route. No matter how many wrong turns I take, the GPS reroutes me. So even if we decide to take a right turn where God anticipated a left turn (free will), I'm sure he can and does foresee these decisions and reworks his plan as well. God certainly knows what we are worrying about, just as my wife and I can often sense the worries of our own children. Psalm 38:9 speaks to this: *"Lord, all my desire is before You; and my sighing is not hidden from You"* (AMPC). And Psalm 26:2 shows us that God will search our hearts and bring to us exactly what we need: *"Examine me, O Lord, and try me; test my heart and my mind"* (AMPC).

Understandably, trusting that God is providing for our voiced and unvoiced needs can be frightening even on the best of days; at least, this is the case for me. I can't tell you how many times I lose confidence that God is providing for me and steering me in the right direction. Sometimes daily, and at other times sixty times an hour—which, in case math isn't your strong suit, is once every minute. Nevertheless, I do believe that God is providing for us, and that He hears our sighs and searches our hearts and minds for our expressed and unexpressed needs and desires even if not voiced openly in prayer. I believe that this is true—do you?

QUESTIONS TO PONDER

1. Reflect on a time when you were aware of your child's needs even before they themselves came to that awareness. Are there times when perhaps you were aware of the needs of multiple children?

2. Think of times you were preparing for situations for your children that were in the near or distant future. If plan A did not work, did you not immediately move on to plan B?

3. Can you think of times where your choices became God's plan B for your life?

How does God answer our prayers?

*And this is the confidence which we have in him,
that if we ask anything according
to his will he hears us.*
(1 John 5:14, RSV)

I ALWAYS THOUGHT PEOPLE WERE BEING EVASIVE OR EVEN flippant when they would tell me that God's answer to prayer is either "yes," "no," "not yet," or "sure, but it won't go the way you think it will." This seemed like a cop-out response: no matter what happened, you could always assume that God had answered your prayer.

The first prayer I ever prayed was at the age of twelve in a tent at a friend's trailer park. I prayed for three thousand dollars for my dad, so we could fix up and continue to live in the house that had been in shambles since my parents' divorce. I never did receive the money; however, a few weeks later I did get removed from my home and placed with friends while my dad entered rehab for alcohol abuse. During this time, my mom was living elsewhere with her new boyfriend, who would eventually become my stepfather.

I have no idea where I came up with that sum of money, or with the idea that God handed out money in the first place. I was not raised to know God in any way, form, or fashion. My family did not attend church except for the rare obligatory Christmas Eve mass. The only symbol of God for me around my house was the huge Catholic church down the street. Looking back now, that church (St. John the Baptist Parish) and its steeple, which was lit up at night, for some reason comforted me many nights as I was walking our neighbourhood streets alone.

It was a busy Saturday morning when my daughter asked me for the third time if we could go to the local indoor water park. I told her—yet again—that I still wasn't sure because there were a few things that I had to take into consideration before I decided. She was obviously impatient with that answer. At the same time, my son was asking me if he could download a new Xbox game after his hockey practice, to which I promptly answered "no." I reminded him about his promise to work harder at school before he could think about purchasing another game. I also had in mind that the last thing I wanted to do was provide a reason for him to cherish more Xbox time at the expense of other things he could be doing that were much better for him physically and for his relationships in general. While conversing with my two oldest children, my youngest son, Luke, was hanging off my leg, asking over and over for some chocolate milk. I poured some chocolate milk for him as I continued to explain to my oldest son my reasoning behind my denial of his request for a new game, and then once again explained to my daughter that I would decide later about the water park and let her know as soon as I did.

Essentially, I delayed an answer for my daughter, responded with a definite no to my oldest son, and affirmed my youngest son's request for chocolate milk almost immediately. Sometimes after I've denied one of my children's requests, they will continue to ask me to change my mind because they don't like the answer, or demand I give a better reason for my denial (I'm sure you've been there too). Sometimes I ignore the redundant requests and demands, telling them that it is a final decision. Many times, after things calm down and I'm tucking them in at night, we can revisit the reasons for my decisions and try to satisfy their unrest, even if their gratification still hungers for satisfaction. I'm sure there are even nights when perceived unfairness, resentment, and anger linger in their minds and hearts as the result of decisions I made. So goes the task of being a loving parent.

I still find it hard to accept that God can answer my prayers by saying "no," "not right now," or "maybe," even as I myself do the same to my own children. Just like my children, I want all yes answers, and if the answer is no, I want God to reconsider over and over. At times, I feel resentment and anger towards God and perceive that he is being unfair, or even ignoring me, just as my children probably at times feel towards me. I would like to think that the decisions I make for my children are backed by solid reasoning, love, and fairness, and always with their ultimate care in mind. Is it not possible that God does just the same for all of us despite our doubt and lack of understanding? Is it not fair to say that God also answers us—sometimes immediately, sometimes with a definite no, and at other times hanging with a maybe or not yet? Unless I'm prepared to call myself a hypocrite I must concede that it is not only possible, but most certainly the case.

QUESTIONS TO PONDER

1. Reflect on times that God answered you with no, yes, or maybe. Can you now see how God's denial, approval, or patience paid off in your life?

2. Right now, what is one request for which you are asking God to reconsider his negative response?

3. Can you think of a situation where you now know absolutely that if you'd gotten what you asked for, it would have had negative consequences for you?

4. Can you recall an event in your life where in retrospect God seemed to have perfect timing and his delay now makes sense?

5. Do you feel any anger or resentment towards God, or feel like he is being or has been unfair to you?

6. Reflect on a time where your resentment or anger turned to gladness or trust after watching events unfold.

How come we can't hear God's voice?

Listen in silence because if your heart is full of other things you cannot hear the voice of God.
—Mother Teresa[9]

THE OTHER NIGHT, MY DAUGHTER ASKED ME WHY SHE couldn't hear God's voice. I knew in my gut that like most of the discussions between my daughter and me, this wasn't going to be an easy conversation, and I wondered if I could give an answer that would leave her with any sense of satisfaction.

Was I fooling myself when it came to hearing God? How did I know I was hearing God's voice and not just my own intuition or inner voice? I have had many talks with God that in the end could have been nothing more than soothing self-talk. How many times have I prayed about my own fears, all the while practicing breathing and mindfulness while thinking logically through things? Is God really on the other end of these prayers, or is the peace that surpasses all understanding just

---

[9] Ruma Bose & Lou Faust, *Mother Teresa, CEO: Unexpected Principles for Practical Leadership* (San Francisco, CA: Berrett-Koehler, 2011), p. 98.

a pacified central nervous system? (I hope it is obvious by now that I do believe prayer with God is much more than self-talk or a calmed nervous system.) This doesn't mean that doubt doesn't enter the picture often—again, sometimes even sixty times an hour—but I remind myself that doubt is often what draws me close to God if I bring it to him and ask for help. Mark 9:24 (RSV) says, *"I believe; help my unbelief."*

In answer to my daughter's question, I told her about the first hours, days, and weeks I spent with her after she was born. I talked about how I used to look into her little ocean eyes telling her how much I loved her, and all the wonderful things I hoped for her future. I pointed out that I was very confident that at that time she didn't understand a word that I spoke to her, but I sensed that she did understand the love in my voice, and that this was very evident to me by her captured gaze and little smirks and smiles. I explained to her that just as she came to understand the English language and was eventually able to comprehend the sounds and words I was uttering to her, she would also come to understand how God speaks to her. God's language will one day cease to be foreign to her. I told her that it was my hope that she and her brothers would begin to understand the ways God is telling each of them that He loves them, what He hopes for them in their future, and that he is always with them.

Another thought came to mind that I shared with my daughter that night. I told her how my wife and I expressed our love for her and her brothers through action just as much as words. Asking my daughter to relax, I asked her to imagine herself as an infant and how she may have taken in all her surroundings and been comforted by the sights, smells, and soft textures all around her. I described how her mom and I prepared a crib, a baby nursery, and warm comfortable clothing before each of our children arrived home. She understood that we did this so that she and her brothers would be comfortable when they came to their new home and would sense that they were safe and loved.

By the smile on my daughter's face, I could tell that this explanation made an impression on her. Did God do the same for us? Perhaps God also spoke through action as he prepared this world with the same love and intention that my wife and I did when we prepared a nursery for each of our children. Could all these amazing sights, smells, wonders, and experiences also have been arranged so that you and I would know that we are loved and cared for? I feel that God did have this in mind, and hoped that it would unquestionably communicate his love for us.

Action can be a powerful form of communication— sometimes even more than words can be. What about actual communication through words, though? At the risk of sounding redundant, reflect back to a time when your children were infants. I bet that you tried really hard to communicate your love for them through your words, and I also bet that you waited in great anticipation for the time when they could actually understand what you were saying to them. Isn't it possible that we also must learn the language of the heart, which is the language God uses to speak to us? I'm certain God's language isn't English. Job 33:14 (ESV) says, *"For God speaks in one way, and in two, though man does not perceive it."* Silence isn't something most of us are good at, or comfortable with, but silence is necessary to hear God as well. The quote by

Mother Teresa at the heading of this chapter reminds us of this. Read it again. Many times in prayer when I feel that I can't hear God's voice, I realize that what I really have to do is stop talking. *"Be still, and know that I am God"* (Psalm 46:10, RSV). Surely, God has also been trying since the day of our birth to communicate his love for us, just as I did when each of my children were placed in my arms. God does this directly with his voice and silent presence. John 10:27 says, *"My sheep hear my voice, and I know them, and they follow me"* (ESV). God also speaks indirectly through the creation that surrounds us. Undoubtedly, God anticipates the time when we will finally recognize his voice, and the many ways that he communicates his love for us.

I also explained to Kara and Luke, who had now climbed into my lap, that God speaks directly to us by his word through the scriptures as well; however, on this night they both decided that sleep was more necessary than reading.

QUESTIONS TO PONDER

1. How do you feel God speaks to us?

2. Can you see how some of the things of this world were prepared for us and our benefit and comfort, communicating God's love?

3. Reflect on how you communicate love to your own children without language, then reflect on how God may be doing the same for you.

4. Do you believe God has communicated with you?

Where is God?

*What can be seen on earth indicates neither the
total absence, nor the manifest presence of divinity,
but the presence of a hidden God.
Everything bears this stamp.*
—Blaise Pascal[10]

AS YOU CAN TELL BY NOW, MY DAUGHTER AND I HAVE HAD many bedtime discussions about God. On another night she wanted to know where God was right at that moment, and why she couldn't see him. I thought this was going to be a tougher question to answer, until I thought about the hide and seek games we often play. (I reiterate that no metaphor is perfect. Perfection is not a requirement of metaphors to lead us to understanding.)

One day while playing hide and seek in our house, I climbed up on the clothes dryer and snuck out the basement window. I then watched with amusement as my three children desperately searched for me in the house. They looked in every room, calling my name numerous times, only to come up

[10] Thomas V. Morris, *Making Sense of It All: Pascal and the Meaning of Life* (Grand Rapids, MI: Wm. B. Eerdmans Publishing, 1992), p. 94.

empty in their search. They were truly perplexed. My little son Luke was even looking under pillows on our downstairs couch. I still laugh about this to this day.

As funny as this was, a serious point came to mind while I watched them search aimlessly for me that day. The pictures of me on the walls, my guitars, the shelving and trim work I'd installed were all signs of my workings and presence, yet I myself was nowhere to be found in the house. There were signs of my existence everywhere and yet I wasn't there in the house with them. I think this raises an interesting point: do we not also search for God in this physical world expecting to find him? We look under all the pillows and search the whole house only to come up empty, just like my children did. But what if God is actually outside of his created universe, just like I was outside of my house the day my children and I played hide and seek? My children could see the signs of my existence everywhere within the house, but I was nowhere to be found.

Eventually it dawned on my older son that I must have snuck out of the house. He realized that I must have gone outside somehow—that was the only explanation that made sense to him as to why I couldn't be found. (Many great theologians and philosophers have come to the same conclusion regarding God's absence in our world.) I heard my son suggest this to my daughter and younger son. As they were discussing this possibility, I crawled back in through the window, surprising them all.

The signs of God's existence can be seen everywhere in and around the home we call earth, just as they are evident in the universe in its entirety. When we see the beauty and organized structure of the world—a blazing sunset, the miracle of women's body growing a baby—or experience the insurmountable complexity of the biological sciences, we naturally ponder these signs of God's workings and creativity. St. Paul put it straightforwardly in Romans 1:20 (NIV): *"For since the creation of the world God's invisible qualities—his eternal power and divine nature—have been clearly seen, being understood by what was made, so that people are without excuse."* If we look for God "inside the house," we will not find him walking around in our gardens, because he has stepped out (for good reasons, which we will get to later).

Now, obviously my children had direct knowledge of my existence before our little game of hide and seek; however, it is conceivable that a stranger could walk into my home and learn plenty about my existence and character without ever meeting me. They could gain this knowledge simply by taking a stroll through my house and by observing the various things within it. The personal touches of certain aspects of the home, as well as the testimony of my wife and children of my ongoing presence, would lend credibility to my existence. Nevertheless, it would still be possible that after all of this information and evidence of my existence was presented, this same person could deny that Kevin Jarvis is a real person that actually lives there in the house. They could deny it because they themselves had not seen me in person living there, despite the insurmountable evidence that I did.

This, I believe, is how a believer and an atheist read the evidence of this world. "This man's slippers are left by the door, you say, and yet he is nowhere to be found," says the atheist. "He just stepped out briefly and will return soon," says the believer. As to why God stepped out in the first place, we will examine that next.

QUESTIONS TO PONDER

1. Reflect on the things in the world that lend credence to God's existence for you.

2. Can you see how others can conclude that God is not home (does not exist)? How do you reconcile this?

3. Do you feel that there is enough evidence in the universe for God's existence without seeing him?

4. Reflect on what things make you doubt that God is home at all. Can you find reason to argue against those conclusions?

5. Are you able to accept that God is, in fact, outside of the universe and yet still very present? Does this sit well with you or create unease?

Why does God remain outside of the world?

If God exists, why doesn't he make his existence more obvious, such that it could not rationally be doubted?
—Travis Dumsday[11]

ON WEDNESDAY MORNINGS, THE GARBAGE COLLECTION comes early in our neighbourhood. I was downstairs with my kids one morning when I heard the familiar sound of air brakes and the deep rumble of the garbage truck just down the road from our house. I realized I'd forgotten to take the garbage to the road, so I looked at my son, making sure I caught his attention.

Looking him right in the eye, I said to him with a hint of rhetorical spice, "You're in charge for a few minutes while I take the garbage out; keep everyone safe, and no fighting please."

My son replied, "Sure, Dad."

Out I went to gather the garbage. On my second trip down the driveway, I heard the all-too-familiar protesting scream of

---

[11] John E. Bowers, *One Priest's Wondering Beliefs: Progressive Christianity: A Critical Review of Christian Doctrines* (Eugene, OR: Wipf and Stock, 2016), p. 155.

my daughter, followed by the familiar sound of crying as she voiced her complaint, "I want it back."

As I got back to the house, I stood close to the door so I could hear what the argument was about. I could hear my son telling my daughter that she'd taken something that wasn't hers in the first place. My daughter shot back that he didn't have to punch her in the back, though. Little four-year-old Luke, playing referee, mediated with his little plaintive voice, "No hurt Kara Owen." All-out mayhem is perhaps a dramatic description, but if you have kids, you get the picture. When I walked in, I calmed the situation as all three attempted to plead their case. The point? Unsupervised responsibility. That is what I'm getting at here. The decision to give my son the responsibility I did while I briefly stepped out ultimately could be seen as a trial of his ability to act responsibly and his willingness to be held accountable when not in the shadow of my presence.

What if after handing him this responsibility I had stayed in the house, and in the very same room? Would the responsibility I'd bestowed on my son not have been somewhat muted? I think it would have. He would not have had a chance to rise to the occasion with me standing over and beside him, and if he did act responsibly, it would have been a half effort, knowing I was standing close by to reprimand him if he decided against his sworn duty. He would also have confidence that I would intervene to stop any wrongdoing if things got out of hand, which also would undermine his sense of accountability. It's kind of like drivers who go the speed limit when being followed by a cop. They aren't choosing not to speed; they're choosing not to experience the consequences of speeding.

I appreciate that we're not talking about murder, rape, a mass shooting, or organizing the holocaust here; however, as in the case of the caterpillar and butterfly mentioned previously, we must distinguish between how and why human responsibilities are bestowed upon our children, and why God bestows such responsibilities on us. As a human parent I can "leave the room" to allow my children to take responsibility for themselves and others, and for the working out of small moral dilemmas, yet God can "leave the room" to allow for ultimate moral responsibility for ourselves and others, true compassion, courage, and the working out of moral dilemmas that may even involve life or death decisions. In fact, if we are to truly develop or act on any of the virtues most of us deeply admire, then God must leave us to ourselves. So, perhaps God leaves the room, or in modern theological terms, remains hidden for our benefit. Perhaps God realized that the only way for any of his children to develop any true moral responsibility would be in his absence, without him standing over and beside us, therefore avoiding obligatory moral action, which isn't true moral valour at all. God remains hidden so that our true moral fibre can be seen both by God and ourselves. God stepping out of the room is the only way for him to truly bestow any amount of real moral accountability on us, ultimately distinguishing true saints from compliant sinners.

QUESTIONS TO PONDER

1. Do you think that if God was "in the room" the way you treat others and yourself might change?

2. Can you think of a time one of your children surprised you with authentic virtue while you were "out of the room"? How did it make you feel?

3. Reflect on how the hiddenness of God may perhaps be a good thing for our overall character and virtue development.

Is God a psychological projection?

You can't convince a believer of anything; for their belief is not based on evidence, it's based on a deep seated need to believe.
—Carl Sagan[12]

I CANNOT TELL YOU HOW MANY TIMES I HAVE HEARD atheists explain to me that belief in God is nothing more than a father complex projected onto an imaginary God above. They also claim that these projected beliefs are probably largely unconscious and therefore not entirely our fault, bringing upon us sympathy rather than blame. This very simple explanation is often seen to be a silver bullet argument for the atheists, plain as the nose on your face.

Another line of argument that they often take to undermine faith in God is attempting to show that religious beliefs are all the result of our culture and family environment. An atheist friend of mine once explained to me in a rather lengthy

---

[12] Judson Poling, *Do Science and the Bible Conflict?* (Grand Rapids, MI: Zondervan, 2003), p. 21.

discourse that I'm only a Christian because I was raised in a predominantly Christian culture with a predominantly Catholic family heritage. Truth be told, yes, I do live in a culture with an overwhelmingly Christian tradition; however, even though my family background is Catholic, I was not brought up in the faith at all. My family is far from what you would call practicing Catholics. I came to faith through reason and intellect and self-motivated philosophical and theological studies throughout my early twenties.

This line of reasoning raises a contradiction though. If I'm a Christian only because of my cultural and familial background, then aren't the atheist's beliefs a result of their own personal and cultural backgrounds as well? If you were to live in a part of Europe that is predominantly atheist then couldn't I explain your atheism the same way you explain my Catholicism—as a custom, or a molding of your belief system based on cultural immersion?

The reality is that there are many people raised as atheists who ultimately become theists, and still others raised as theists who become atheists. We believe or do not believe in God based on emotion, intellect, and experience, as well as familial and cultural background, which are different for everyone. Our background should not be used as the final determinant of truth concerning our beliefs. Our faculties of intellect, emotion and cognition play a role as well. These faculties can and do often lead us to truth, though a truth that is independent of those very faculties, our cultural background, and intellectual judgement of the facts.

Like most things in life, some of us get it right and some of us get it wrong. The fact that some people believe God exists, while others don't, in no way changes whether he exists or not. I can argue all day long why I believe atheists are wrong; however, if there is an emotional reason for their unbelief, then no amount of this intellectual jousting will make any difference in the end. It is this emotional aspect of belief that I want to address.

One afternoon my youngest son (three-and-a-half at the time) came into the kitchen asking for a fruit bar—which would have been his second one that day. I told him that he couldn't have it. This sent him into a rage. He started to cry, telling me that I wasn't his dad anymore and he didn't love me and he wanted a new daddy. He ran to his room and covered himself up on his bed. He tried again to get me to give in to his request, but the same answer was followed by the same type of tantrum and tears. I tried to comfort him and explain why I wouldn't give him another bar, but this had no positive effect on him. He went back into his room for the next twenty minutes and refused to talk with me.

I admit that it hurt to hear those words, though most parents have heard things like this from their children at one time or another. I allowed him his space. While I was sitting alone in my room, I heard his footsteps. Without a word, he climbed into my lap. I hugged him tightly. I told him how much I loved him as he rested his head on my shoulder, and he told me that I could be his daddy again and that he loved me too.

I couldn't help but wonder if this experience could teach me anything about my relationship with God—or, for that matter, about other people's relationship with God. What was my son really saying with his hurtful words and through his tears? I knew he loved me and didn't really want a new daddy.

Thinking back, I'm pretty positive my son was saying a few things: that he wasn't happy with not getting his own way, that he felt betrayed, and that he wanted to be his own boss and live by his own rules. In his emotional state, my son seemed to decide that if he lashed out at me, maybe I would change my mind, or if he disowned or hurt me, then perhaps my rules would also go away and he could do whatever he wanted.

Simple explanations for faith in God from atheists are accepted like profound truth that have come about by equally profound insight. How's this for simple? Perhaps atheists deny God firstly in the hope that they will then be free to do their own bidding, shedding themselves of what seems to them to be unnecessary burdens and obligation, and secondly in an effort to rid themselves of the rule-maker that seems unnecessarily restraining and stern. Just as my wish for God to exist may in the end be nothing more than an unconscious projection for an all-powerful protective father, couldn't the atheist be engaging in the same unconscious projection in reverse? Could the atheist, at bottom, be wishing that there is not an all-powerful God that makes moral demands, challenges our selfish desires, and has expectations of us?

My son eventually gave up his rebellion and returned to me. Presumably the atheist should do the same. Of course, they could always choose to continue to live in blindness to their own unconscious projections, and this would elicit more sympathy rather than blame.

QUESTIONS TO PONDER

1. How do you feel when you hear that your faith is nothing more than a projected wish?

2. Reflect on a time one of your children rebelled against one of your rules or demands.

3. Can you remember a time you rebelled against God?

4. What wish or idea do you feel was behind your rebellion?

Why all the rules and boundaries?

See in the meantime that your faith brings forth obedience, and God in due time will cause it to bring forth peace.
—John Owen[13]

AROUND THE AGE OF TWELVE, MY PARENTS DECIDED TO divorce after years of fighting and general turmoil. My mother left our family one evening during dinner in what seemed like a split-second decision. The weeks and months dragged on. My mother did not return. My brother and I were left with my dad, who at the time was fighting an escalating battle with the bottle and losing, and he and I were often left alone to fend for ourselves. Most days we managed to put together something for breakfast and dinner. With no consistent supervision, we both decided on a day-to-day basis if we did or didn't want to attend school. In the evenings, I was free to do whatever I wanted because I didn't have anyone there to enforce a curfew, tell me to take a shower, or get me ready for bed. Often, I would find myself wandering the

---

[13] John Owen, *A Practical Exposition on the 130th Psalm* (British Library, 1830), p. 414.

streets of our neighbourhood, trying to find something to do or someone to hang out with. During the school year, the streetlights coming on meant dinner time and night routine for most of the kids in my neighbourhood. For me, the streetlights meant more freedom to continue to do whatever I wanted to do. I could ride my bike, play video games, or watch a movie.

Ironically it was at these times I felt the loneliest, especially as I walked by the houses of my friends. From the sidewalks, I could see the television flickering in their living rooms, or their families gathering around their dinner tables. The comforting smell of laundry dryer exhaust vents still haunts me to this day. For some reason, that smell reminded me of the comfort and safety I didn't have. I mention all of this because I can remember several times when different friends would protest the unfairness of their parents calling them in for the night or home for dinner when I got to stay out for as long as I wanted. One of my friends, after learning that I didn't have to be in the house at any particular time, told me how lucky I was and how jealous he was of my lack of rules.

I felt anything but lucky. I felt lost, abandoned, and desperate for someone to take control. How could my friends understand that the rules and boundaries that their parents set for them and did their best to enforce were anything but unfair? How could I expect them to see that those very ordinances were a sign of love and protection? In truth, I didn't understand this either until much later in my life. I can't tell you how many times my children protest limited screen time, a shower before bed, or a curfew on school nights. Homework is a whole other issue. I have watched my kids throw tantrums when I ask them to clean up after themselves or eat a healthy snack before bed instead of junk food. These things are done out of love and protection for them.

I make these demands to help them grow and learn; however, my children sometimes see them as unfair expectations or unreasonable rules enforced by a tyrannical parent.

How many people do we know that deem God to be a tyrannical parent as well? Perhaps even you have seen him in this light at times. It's popular in our society to describe God's commandments and principles for living as outdated and unreasonable. But can't we see how God could be protecting us and loving us by creating boundaries, expectations, and principles for living? I once heard it said that we don't break God's rules so much as we break ourselves by ignoring God's rules. When God hands down commandments about our sexuality, how we should treat ourselves and each other, or how to generally live an honest and selfless life, can't we see that he is being loving like any good parent should be? We put in place all kinds of rules and boundaries for our own children, but when God does the same for us we accuse his love as being outdated and out of touch with reality.

My parents and I have reconciled and healed our relationship, but the negative messages I buried in myself about not being worthy of care and attention are wounds I still work to heal. The emptiness of abandonment still haunts me to this day, and it is something I continue to work through. I also struggle with roles that demand responsibility from me, because I had too much freedom and unlimited boundaries as a kid. We may protest God's love for us in the form of demands, commandments, and principles of living; however, may we never forget that not demanding, correcting, or guiding is not loving at all. In the end we find that rules and boundaries are really love in disguise, and can love really ever be outdated?

QUESTIONS TO PONDER

1. Can you think of rules or guidelines that God has placed on you that make you feel uncomfortable?

2. Ask yourself honestly: if these restrictions were lifted from you, what would result? Would there be positive or negative consequences for you or the people in your life?

3. Reflect on a time you broke yourself by disobeying one of God's rules or commands.

4. Can you think of rules and boundaries you set for your own children that they rebel against or perceive as unfair?

5. How do you feel when your children go beyond the set boundaries or intentionally ignore your restrictions?

6. Reflect on how God may be caring for you and others in your life by restricting your unbridled passions.

If God knows our choices ahead of time, are we free?

*Almightiness and wisdom combined
will make no mistakes.*
—Charles Haddon Spurgeon[14]

I ALWAYS STRUGGLED WHEN PEOPLE WOULD TELL ME THAT God plans for our mistakes, can foresee when and where we will go wrong, and then works things out for the best. God's complete sovereignty has always left me a little itchy under the collar. How can God know what we will do in advance of our freewill decisions? This has always seemed like a contradiction and left me feeling like my decisions were somehow cheapened, or that they were wholly predetermined. It is a struggle for me to understand the theology of God's total sovereignty over our lives while still allowing for our free will, because I don't like the implications that my life is already completely mapped out. Arguably, I do exhibit some sovereignty over my children's lives, but I also understand that they are still ultimately free to

---

[14] Charles Haddon Spurgeon, *Morning and Evening Daily Devotions* (Christian Classics Ethereal Library, 1948), n.p.

make their own choices and decisions. How can we reconcile the sovereignty God has over our lives while still maintaining our freedom? I wondered if I could find a clue within my own experience of being a father.

I began to see that if put to the test, I could predict with a very high degree of accuracy what choices my children would make in various situations. For example: if you were to place a bowl of seedless grapes and a bowl of sliced apples in front of my daughter, I could almost guarantee you that she would choose the grapes. On the other hand, my oldest son would choose the apples, and my youngest son would refuse both and ask for cookies. If my daughter was presented with the option of playing video games or choreographing dance routines, I can once again predict with high accuracy that she would choose to dance. My youngest son would forgo both options in favour of going off and playing by himself.

Regarding the choice between cookies and apples, I also know what isn't good for my children, and understand that if given the option of cookies along with the apples and grapes, the outcome would be written in stone. If I placed three brownies in the mix, then all three of my children would forgo the healthy choices and immediately devour the less nutritious snack every time. My job as a parent is to put forth as many healthy options as possible based on each of their unique likes and tastes, while at the same time limiting the unhealthy choices. I know with a high degree of accuracy what they prefer in most cases, so I present options that are good for them and try to limit the bad options. Does God not do the same for us?

Granted, a one-time snack is a small choice without much consequence; however, the point remains. If I can prepare grapes instead of apples for my daughter based on what I know about her and what she will most probably choose, then is it not possible that God could do the same for us based on his intimate knowledge and understanding of our character?

Jeremiah 1:5 (NIV) says, *"Before I formed you in the womb I knew you."* At the end of the day, I may be preparing grapes instead of apples, or hiding the brownies, but God may be preparing for us and presenting options concerning our life experiences, relationships, and career paths, as well as steering us away from temptations and lusts beyond our powers to resist. Surely, God plans on leading us to the good things in life based on our unique likes and tastes, and at the same time tries to limit the bad things for our own good.

Once again: I know my children in a finite way. God knows us in infinite ways, and that is the difference that ultimately makes all the difference. Perhaps God's sovereignty over our lives is based more on intimate knowledge of who and what we are rather than constant interference with our free will. Complete sovereignty now sounds a lot more like love than hard determinism, doesn't it?

QUESTIONS TO PONDER

1. Reflect on how intimately you know your own children, and how you foresee certain situations happening for them and plan ahead.

2. Can you think of a time that God apparently planned ahead for you?

3. Is there a time when you asked God for cookies and he ended up giving you carrots?

4. Do you believe God is sovereign over your life?

How does God comfort us?

*Cast all your anxiety on him
because he cares for you.*
(1 Peter 5:7, NIV)

I HAVE STRUGGLED WITH ANXIETY FOR MUCH OF MY LIFE. The most difficult times were when I felt God was not listening to me, or that he was flat out refusing to help me. Many times, prayer seemed like I was talking to a wall or, as C.S. Lewis once described it, "posting letters to a non-existent address."[15]

It was just a normal afternoon at the arena chasing around my daughter and youngest son after my oldest son's hockey game—that is, until my daughter went tumbling down eight concrete steps in the lobby of the arena. I'd forgotten how quickly I could jump into action and how much spring in my step I still had until I practically leaped the first steps up to the landing where she was laying. She immediately reached out for me, crying. I'll never forget how scared she looked. She had

---

[15] Perry C. Bramlett, *C.S. Lewis: Life at the Center* (Macon, GA: Smyth & Helwys Publishing, 1996), p. 54.

two or three goose eggs on her head, but otherwise seemed okay. After looking over her wounds with the help of a paramedic friend that happened to be in the arena, we headed home. She was still upset, but started to calm considerably as I reassured her.

After taking a warm bath, she crawled up on my lap in the rocking chair. As I was playing with her hair, I could see that the goose eggs were considerably reduced but still quite visible. She was completely settled now, nestled in my arms.

At that moment, it struck me that despite my daughter's physical hurts, what I was really doing was calming her fears, not healing her physical wounds. No matter how much I comforted my daughter that day, her physical wounds would remain for some time. There have been so many of these bumps, scrapes, mishaps, and cuts throughout the years I have lost count.

I've experienced my own share of bumps, bruises, and scrapes, too. One day when I was about six years old, my brother and I were swinging golf clubs out in front of our house. My brother accidently swung the club too far on the back swing and hit me in the top of the forehead. I will never forget the warm feeling of blood running down my face and the sheer terror I felt. My brother ran for help, and I froze in fear. The next thing I remember was sitting on my mother's lap in our family car on the way to the hospital. I can remember calming down as my mom and dad reassured me that everything was going to be okay, despite feeling blood in my ears and trickling down my cheeks. A horrible and painful situation to be sure, but ultimately my parents' reassurance and presence stopped this scenario from becoming all-out suffering in terror and anxiety.

Philippians 4:7 (RSV) speaks about a peace that *"passes all understanding"* coming over us, no matter what circumstances may be playing out in our lives. This passage is clearly describing God's presence enveloping us during many different trials in our lives, both physical and psychological. God asks us to give him our worries, as St. Peter reminds us: *"Cast all your anxieties on him, for he cares about you"* (1 Peter 5:7, RSV). These verses do not say that God will always heal our ills or rectify a horrible situation so we can experience peace. What these verses do say is that even *during* these trials and tribulations, we will experience this peace. In just the same way that I comforted my daughter without healing her wounds, and just as my parents comforted me in my time of fear, will God not do the same for us if we turn to Him? A "peace that passes all understanding" implies that we won't be able to understand how we can feel peaceful amid any amount of suffering; however, we often do.

QUESTIONS TO PONDER

1. Reflect on a time when you felt God comfort you in your heart and mind despite a physical/earthly challenge.

2. Have you ever experienced the peace that surpasses all understanding during life situations that evoked tremendous anxiety?

3. Do you need to turn to God for comfort because of a specific situation in your life right now?

4. Can you accept that God may be comforting you despite an ongoing challenge in your life?

How does God work through others?

*Do not make the Great Commission
your Great Omission.*
—Daryl Baugh[16]

WORKING IN LAW ENFORCEMENT FOR THE PAST FIFTEEN years, I've learned a few things about the different aspects of the job, and one of the most challenging roles is that of the dispatcher.

The dispatcher is the person pulling all the strings behind the scenes. They are busy prioritizing calls, routing the number of officers and assigning backup as well as monitoring the location of all patrol units in the city. One night while patrolling, I was listening to the radio transmissions when I heard that a woman was in a certain area of the city threatening to commit suicide. In such a situation, the dispatcher immediately determines which units are closest and available and then promptly sends those units, along with other first responders, to the scene. Once they hear the call, other units can also decide

---

[16] Available at https://www.goodreads.com/author/quotes/14841592.Daryl_Baugh.

to assist on their own even without being assigned. If the call is serious enough, other units usually choose to respond, but of course there are units that decide not to attend for various reasons, some of which are legitimate and others that seem to lack all compassion.

I remember driving around that cold night, a light flurry of snow wisping over the streets. I was reflecting on how this woman's life could depend on how compassionate and motivated the officers and first responders dispatched to find her were. Several hours later, there were multiple units searching for this girl. It was a team effort, and thankfully it was ultimately successful. The officers dispatched to the call refused to give up on finding her and ensuring her safety. The dispatcher was working just as hard coordinating the effort. In fact, some dispatchers I know say that their job can pose more emotional difficulties than front line officers face. In this case, as a front-line officer, I was busy actively looking for the girl that needed help, but the dispatcher was essentially waiting for others to find and help her. The tension in such cases can be palpable. The dispatcher can often be on the phone with a distraught, terrified, or injured person the whole time it takes for first responders to get to the scene. Most people speak of time flying, but I can assure you that it often crawls.

When I was making my way back to the station that night, I couldn't help thinking how the dispatcher might be a great metaphor for how God works through others for our benefit. Replace the missing girl with any one of God's children, which is to say you or me. Perhaps God is the greatest dispatcher there is. When we reach out to God for help through prayer, maybe he looks at the location of all the available help in the area and puts the call out, just like an emergency dispatcher. How many times have I cried out to God for help in the silence of my heart, or through my wordless tears, only to have a friend call at the perfect hour, or a book recommendation come at the perfect time, or have a chance run in with a wise leader within the community?

Looking back, I can think of many of my own experiences where I can see God at work behind the scene. He himself stays on the line and supports us as the responders make their way to the scene. I feel that God has done this many times for me. Maybe God uses thoughts, promptings of our conscience, and intuition to affect our wills instead of the phones and radios used by emergency dispatchers. I think God appoints us all the role of first responder and hopes we will answer the call when it comes to us; however, as you know, some choose not to respond at all. And again, I believe that God stays on the line with us through prayer, and tries to help us through our terror and calm our fears as he waits along with us for available units to arrive.

If we think back to our discussion about how God can anticipate and provide for our expressed and unexpressed needs, the metaphor of the dispatcher also fits. Sometimes even before receiving a call for service, dispatchers will send officers to certain parts of the city in hopes of preventing possible emergency situations from evolving. They also send units to check on the wellbeing of vulnerable people in the community. Isn't this what God does by sending all of us out to minister to those in need and provide for those who cannot help themselves, and by commissioning us to love one another as he has loved us?

Presumably, just like a dispatcher, God would rather prevent emergencies in our lives than respond to them. That being said, I'm pretty confident that when the next emergency rears up in my life, God is definitely the dispatcher I want assigning and routing the first responders and staying on the line with me until help arrives.

QUESTIONS TO PONDER:

1. Can you think of a time you prayed to God for help and you were convinced that a person or experience was the result of that prayer?

2. Reflect on times you felt God was prompting you to help someone, make a call, or offer resources. Did you answer the prompt?

3. Can you see how God could and would use others to help you, comfort you, and lead you?

4. Do you remember a time when God stayed on the line with you when you were terrified or distraught? Did this make a difference for you?

Why natural evil?

There is nothing evil but what is within us; the rest is either natural or accidental.
—Philip Sidney[17]

IN A PREVIOUS CHAPTER, WHEN I SPOKE ABOUT GOD preparing the world like a parent prepares a nursery, it raises an obvious question: If God prepared all the beauty and wonder we see in the world, then why did he also create (or allow) horror, tragedy, loss, and suffering? Maybe God didn't do such a great job of preparing the nursery after all. One only has to think of mosquitoes, poisonous spiders, or tornados to raise reasonable doubts whether God's provision for us is truly benevolent.

When my wife and I built our home, we tried to make it the safest, coziest and most practical home we could. We had electrical outlets put in all the right places, stairs allowing us access to both levels, furniture for comfort, plumbing for running

---

[17] Sir Philip Sidney & Jane Porter, *Aphorisms of Sir Philip Sidney: With Remarks* (London: Longman, Hurst, Rees & Orme, 1807), p. 136.

water, and a heating and cooling system for climate control. Many other logistics were factored into the overall design and build of our home. My wife and I took into consideration all the comfort, practicalities, and necessities we could think of. In time, the home was complete. Overall, we were proud of it, and believed it to be the safe, comfortable, and practical home we set out to make it in the first place.

I believe God did the same with the earth, and I also believe that God knew—just as my wife and I discovered—that avoiding all potential dangers of living in a physical space was not possible. In the home we built, the stairs that lead to the lower level are the same stairs that my son smashed his knee on. The couch placed in the lower level for comfort is the same couch from which my daughter jumped off onto her brother, sending him screaming. The electrical outlets throughout the home always run the risk of shock or fire. The heating and cooling system could malfunction, leaving us in extreme cold or sweltering heat.

In the case of a severe malfunction, it's entirely possible that these utilities and systems could cause catastrophic injury or death. Electrical outlets can pose a danger when used improperly. A heating and cooling system that is abused or incorrectly maintained can break down. Stairs can easily become hazards when toys are left on them carelessly. These are just a few examples of an endless list of things that could go wrong in the building and furnishing of a home. If any one of my kids decided to leave the hot water running all day while I was at work, wouldn't I eventually have a water heater problem? If they left the furnace cranked without care, wouldn't it eventually affect the system, as well as lead to collateral damage such as spoiled food or damaged windows from condensation? What if my children decided to ignore my lessons about the danger of electricity and stuck silverware in the outlets? What would happen if the windows were left open on a snowy winter day? I can visualize what our home would look like if we decided together as a family that a clean house was no longer necessary, and we never vacuumed, dusted, or cleaned the toilets. Would there be consequences? Perhaps more viruses leading to illness?

Have we treated the environment God prepared for us properly and with care? I don't think we have. I'm not saying that all natural evil can be explained away as misuse of resources, but a fair bit can. Perhaps God did create the world to provide in the most beneficial way for our comfort, safety, and practical use, and He expected us to use and enjoy the world and the things in it properly and for their intended purpose. If we went back a few hundred years, how pristine would the air, water, and soil have been? Who has polluted and ravaged these resources? Who is to blame for the millions of tons of chemical waste dumped into our lakes and oceans every day of every year? Who has overloaded the vast majority of our food sources with chemicals and pesticides? Which species is responsible for the air pollution that is so prevalent throughout the developed world?

There are many more examples of how human beings have misused, exploited, and ravaged the natural resources provided to us. Have we not taken the home prepared for us and corrupted it in a million ways?

God would have to drastically alter the world as we know it to prevent all natural catastrophes. Perhaps God should have created a world where the ingredients for alcohol or opioids did not exist, therefore preventing all drunk driving accidents and opioid overdoses. While he was at it, he may as well have made it impossible for metal to be manipulated or for heat combustion to be harnessed, therefore eliminating the manufacturing of the cars or airplanes that cause so many fatal accidents. It would have been especially useful to prevent the tinkering with chemicals and genetics that has led to the production of pesticides and artificial foods that are suspected to cause so much cancer and disease.

We could go on forever with examples like this. We can come up with all kinds of ways we feel God could have done a better job, just as I'm sure my own kids could come up with all kinds of ideas about how I could have made our home better and safer. But we must remember that for each of these resources we eliminate, we don't only lose the negative effects that come from their misuse, but the positive experiences that they afford us as well. Try to picture a world with no cars, airplanes, or genetic medicine. In some ways it might be better; however, it is obvious that in other ways it would not. I can imagine suggestions that would come if asked my four-year-old son how I could make our home a safer and more comfortable place. Eliminating certain aspects of our physical space or changing nature's laws would have far-reaching consequences (cause and effect). Can you fathom all of the chain reactions that would result from the alterations you would make if you suddenly had infinite power, given your limited knowledge and experience of the intricacies of the universe? In St. Paul's letter to the Corinthians he writes, *"For who has understood the mind of the Lord so as to instruct him?"* (1 Corinthians 2:16, ESV). Maybe we should trust that God knows what he is doing and not get too big for our britches here.

QUESTIONS TO PONDER

1. Reflect on how we as a human family have abused and not properly cared for the systems and resources bestowed upon us.

2. Think of the work you put into providing a safe home for your own children, and how they could freely choose to ignore warnings or guidelines that would lead to disaster.

3. Overall, do you think God has succeeded or failed in his efforts to provide a safe and secure home for us?

4. What do you feel God could have done differently?

How can God love six billion children?

*He determines the number of the stars
and calls them each by name.*
(Psalm 147:4, NIV)

ONE DECEMBER EVENING, MY WIFE AND I WERE FLYING into Atlanta airport for a connecting flight after a vacation in the Dominican Republic. When we were a couple thousand feet from landing, I couldn't help but notice below me how human civilization looked like a colony of ants hastily going about their business. City lights and headlights neatly lined the highways. I saw tall buildings lit up like giant Christmas trees, what appeared to be endless tractor trailers lining an outdoor warehouse, and plenty of emergency lights flashing up and down the highways. The chaotic yet organized frenzy spoke to me, pulling me into a sense of my own insignificance. I felt emptiness as I contemplated my place in the grand scheme of things. This was only one city in one country of the entire world. The next thought I had was how could God love each one of the six billion or so people on our planet unconditionally, even while a large number of them were not even giving him a passing thought or consideration? Once again, I turned to the love of my own children for an answer.

When my wife gave birth to our first son, Owen, my heart really did feel like it would burst. I couldn't imagine being able to love anyone or anything as much as I loved him. I was overwhelmed with feelings of deep love, and couldn't stop holding him or thinking about him when I wasn't with him. I finally understood why other people with children had never been able to adequately verbalize their feelings towards their children.

Fast forward two and a half years, when my daughter Kara came along. My heart once again grew and felt like it would explode with overwhelming affection, but it didn't; it just grew to make room for even more of this profound love. When my third child, Luke, was born, this process repeated itself with ever-expanding love, and if my wife and I were to have a fourth child I'm sure my heart would again make room.

One night when taking a walk, I thought of a friend of mine who learned that he and his wife were expecting their eighth child. I was struck with the following insight. If I, as a finite being, could make room for three or five or conceivably even *eight* children and still love them all unconditionally, how many more children could an infinite God love? God's love is infinite, and therefore whether God has one child or six billion children, he could love them all deeply and unconditionally, just as I love my own three children and my friend loves his eight children. God's heart would go on forever expanding with every new arrival.

I have friends and family with various numbers of children. Some of those children have grown to be successful, God-serving people, while others are still struggling to find their way in this world. But the parents of the struggling children consistently say that they wouldn't change a thing. They swear that the love they have for their children will never waver, no matter what comes of their individual successes or failures, and they vow that their love for each of their children is completely unconditional and not in any way changed by number or circumstance.

Thankfully, I no longer wonder what this love for a child feels like, and I also know that number or circumstance will not in any way alter the unconditional love I extend to all three of my children. Is it not possible that God feels the same about each and every one of us?

QUESTIONS TO PONDER

1. Reflect on how you felt when each of your children were born. Did the love for each additional child lessen or waver?

2. If you are a new parent, can you imagine how with more children your love will grow and not diminish?

3. Reflect on a time you felt insignificant or invisible to God. Do you think this was true, or possibly a reflection of how your own parents made you feel?

4. If you have more than one child, can you measure your love as more or less towards one or the other?

Does God care for us more than his other creations?

Consider the ravens: they neither sow nor reap, they have neither storehouse nor barn, and yet God feeds them. Of how much more value are you than the birds!
(Luke 12:24, RSV)

I HAVE HAD MANY PETS, MY FAVOURITE BEING A BLACK Labrador dog named Spud. Spud was a best friend to me. I trained him myself, and he was so well-trained that I could take him everywhere without a leash. After many years together, Spud got sick, and as some dogs do when they get sick, he ran away. He ended up in the pound for stray dogs. I didn't learn of this until it was too late, and unfortunately, they euthanized him as an unclaimed stray. I was devastated, to say the least. I have had birds, frogs, gerbils, cats, and fish throughout the years, all with special names, toys, and food, but not one of them was as special as Spud.

Today our family has a betta fish named Oz. We feed Oz and watch her swim around, and sometimes she even takes food from the tip our fingers. I've grown to really like her, and dare I say I love Oz in the sense that I care for her, enjoy her, and want the best for her. When she goes belly-up one day, I'm sure we will all be saddened, especially my daughter. The sadness I felt when learning about Spud was deep and painful as well, and I remember it vividly.

Just as I can have a betta fish, a dog, or a cat in my family home and love them all specially and in different degrees, by no means do I love any of those pets on the same level as my own children. Being a father has now opened me up to a deeper love, as any parent can attest. I have never really appreciated when people say things like, "I know what you are going through with your sick child; I have a fur baby of my own that was sick last week," or "I'm training my puppy right now, so I totally get the lack of sleep and frustration you're experiencing." Sorry to say, but no you don't.

As someone who has experienced deep love for a pet, having a human child and being the owner of a family pet are not the same. The former is a more profound love. This fact does not take away from the special love we feel for our pets, though—I want to make that very clear. I know that love well, and the pain of loss that accompanies it. That being said, when I thought about this further, the following question came to mind. Couldn't God love his other living creations—like birds, whales, elephants and frogs—deeply, and yet still have a special affinity towards his own children created in his image?

I think this is in fact the case. I can easily recall the love I felt for the pets I have had in my life, especially Spud, but when compared to the love I feel for Luke, Kara, and Owen, the difference and degree is unmistakable. God's love and care for his other creations is genuine and special as well. I think this is evident. However, if we were created as sons and daughters of God in his own image, then I think it is obvious that his love for us is also unmistakably different in degree, and ultimately more profound.

QUESTIONS TO PONDER

1. If you are a parent, think about all the pets you have had in your life. Is there a profound difference between how you feel about your children and how you feel (or felt) about your pets?

2. If you are a son or daughter, reflect on how the love your parents have for you may be different than their love for the family pet.

3. Can you see how God may have a special and more profound love for you than his other creations? How does this make you feel?

Can Christianity be truer than other religions?

I believe in Christianity as I believe that the sun has risen: not only because I see it, but because by it I see everything else.
—C.S. Lewis[18]

MANY TIMES, I HAVE HEARD THE ARGUMENT THAT IF TWO men both claim to know God intimately coming from different religious traditions at odds with one another, then one (or both) of the men is either deceived, wrong, or lying. I have taken part in many of these debates or discussions myself. I've learned that when someone is making an argument from personal experience that it is hard to refute their truth, and it may be best to even avoid trying to do so. Still, when I reflect on how my three children can all intimately know me and yet at the same time hold untrue facts or ideas about me, I can see through the apparent contradiction. Here's how. My daughter is of the opinion that I'm a policeman, a professional chef, and her dad.

---

[18] C.S. Lewis, *The Quotable Lewis*, Walter Martindale & Jerry Root, eds. (Wheaton, IL: Tyndale House, 1989), p. 23.

My oldest son knows me as a hockey player, a forty-two-year-old man, a special constable, a hockey coach, and his dad. Then we have my youngest son, who holds the belief that I am his dad as well as a superhero and an astronaut.

Here are the facts. I work a special police constable at a university, I am an okay cook and a hockey player, but I'm not a superhero, a professional chef, or an astronaut. And obviously I am, in fact, a dad to all three of them. With this in mind, I can correct my youngest son's errant view by informing him that I'm not a superhero or astronaut. I can then affirm my daughter's opinion that I am a policeman and her dad, and then confirm my oldest son's knowledge that I am a hockey player, forty-two, and his hockey coach. One of my children (my oldest son in this case) may in fact hold all correct views about me, while another one of my children may insist on believing certain facts about me even if they are in error. Just as one of my children can intimately know me and have more correct knowledge about me than another one of my children, I believe that different religions can be regarded in the same way since they all claim to hold truths about who God is. I believe Christianity is like the child—in this case, my oldest son—who possesses the most correct knowledge about me and yet shares in the intimacy of my presence with the other two children, despite their errant views about who or what I am. These right or wrong assessments may not negate the intimacy my three children share with me in the short term, but they can and do make a difference in the end for a few important reasons.

The errant views of my daughter and youngest son could represent other religions that are misled in their beliefs about who God is. The danger comes when an errant view leads one away from a deeper relationship with God. For instance, if one of my children knows me to be a father that disciplines fairly for wrong behaviour and enforces consequences, while another child of mine believes that I don't much mind wrong or rebellious behaviour, a problem may occur. Maybe one of my children mistakenly believes that the purpose of my existence is to provide for them everything they ever wanted rather than, and more importantly, everything they, in fact, need. This mistaken view may leave them feeling bitter and disappointed with me when their every wish and desire seems to go unsatisfied. Essentially, what we are doing when comparing various religious views is following the law of noncontradiction. The law states that two opposing propositions cannot be true at the same time, and actually are mutually exclusive. Take the following statements: A is B, and A is not B. Obviously, these statements cannot both be true. This law leads us to the fact that not all religious claims can be true at the same time and in the same way.

With all this in mind, is it not possible that Christianity possesses more complete knowledge of who God is and what purpose he has in mind for us than other religions do? Some religions claim that God does not enforce justice, and that Karma takes this role as an impersonal natural law. Some religions declare God to be synonymous with the universe or nature itself, while others maintain God to be a personal being who cares for us deeply. Other religions are certain that God created all things but no longer takes an interest in any of them, while some faiths profess that there are many gods rather than just one. These ideas are contradictory, and therefore cannot all be true in the same way at the same time, because if they were than none of them would be true. They would cancel each other out by way of their contradictory claims.

Ponder that for a moment. Just as all three of my children cannot be right in the same way at the same time if they hold opposing views, doesn't the law of noncontradiction apply for all religions as well? Determining which ideas are true and which are false does make a difference, regardless of what our relativistic culture claims. I don't buy the idea of "true for you but not for me"—do you? In the end, what we believe to be true about God most definitely will affect the way our relationship with him plays out throughout our lives, and will undoubtedly determine whether we spend eternity with him or not, either through choice or consequence.

QUESTIONS TO PONDER

1. Does it make sense to you that not all ideas about God can be true at the same time and in the same way?

2. Can you think of things you may be in error about concerning God's character or nature?

3. Take some time to list some contradictions between various religions. Can they be reconciled?

4. What does Jesus say about God's nature that rings true for you?

5. What about God's nature, if true, would be hard to accept, and why?

Does God care what career we choose?

*Whatever your hand finds to do,
do it with all your might...*
(Ecclesiastes 9:10, NIV)

I ONCE HEARD IT SAID THAT "WHO WE ARE IS A GIFT FROM God, and who we become is gift back to God." I think this is true; however, in our culture it seems that the end phrase has been changed to "How rich and famous we become is a gift back to God."

Using myself as an example, I've tried to prove to everyone for most of my life that I was worthwhile and that I mattered. I wanted the applause of the entire world. When I started to really grow in my relationship with God, I found myself just as committed to trying to prove to God that I was worthwhile as well. Like many others, I have unique gifts and talents, and in some respects, they feel like a burden. Anything I have ever been good at leads me to believe that's what God has destined me to do, and if I fall short, I feel like I'm letting myself and God down. Maybe you can relate!

I'm not exactly sure what God wants me to do with my life. Maybe He wants me to write simple books like this one, or continue writing music. Perhaps public speaking or going back to work for the Church is his plan for me. For all I know, he desires that I stay in my current position at the university, or maybe he wishes that I just continue to be a good father, son, husband, and friend. Clearly, I'm not sure what his plan for my life is, although I'm sure being a good father, son, husband, and friend is part of it.

One day, my daughter Kara asked me what I thought she should be when she grew up. I asked her a question in return: "What do you love to do, Kara?" My daughter proceeded to tell me how she loves art, animals, adventure, and dancing. Of course, I knew these things already. She then told me that one day she would move to Paris and become an artist. What can I say—the kid's got dreams.

I was struck again with an insight. At that moment, I realized that I didn't really have a preference about what she "should do" with her life. At minimum, I wanted her to be a good person who loved others and experienced love in return. I told my daughter that my hope was that she would grow up to be a compassionate and humble person that thinks of others and not only of herself, and that she and I would always remain close.

When all is said and done, I know that I want my daughter to continue to share with me, trust me, and come to me with her hurts and worries. I explained to her that whatever she did in life, that these things were more important to me in the end. I also made it clear that it didn't matter to me whether she became a hairdresser or a pop star. I tried to get her to understand that if we weren't close to one another, and she wasn't a person who cares for herself, others, and God, whatever she did could never make up for those things.

I wondered if God feels the same about us concerning our worldly successes. Did it make a difference to God whether I became a famous musician or a general labourer? Perhaps God cares more that I am a general labourer of my own soul than that I gain worldly success.

Is it possible that all the pressure I put on myself to do something great for God was really another veiled attempt to gain the applause of the world? St. Paul says it best in Galatians 1:10 (NIV): *"Am I now trying to win the approval of human beings, or of God?"* I can imagine that the parents of the latest pop star or professional athlete must be tremendously proud of their children for reaching their goals. However, pop stars and professional athletes also have average siblings—the brother or sister that works a nine to five or is a stay at home mother or father. Are parents any less proud of these "less successful" children? I don't think so.

I love watching my kids explore their gifts and talents because it brings them joy, and it brings me joy to see them have these experiences. Perhaps what God really wants from all of us is that we just enjoy our gifts and talents and try to share them with others when we can. Maybe the quote I mentioned at the beginning of the chapter is true after all; however, how we define "who we become" may make all the difference as to whether we are looking to please others or to please God. I eventually came to understand that not attaining all the worldly success I desired was exactly what allowed me to attain the spiritual growth I learned to desire even more.

I once heard it said that God's purpose for any of us at any given moment is the person on our left, or on our right. Maybe we just overcomplicate matters. In the following chapter, we will explore this in a little more depth.

QUESTIONS TO PONDER

1. What gifts do you feel God has given you?

2. Do you feel that you are using them?

3. Do you feel pressure to do something "big" in life? Why or why not?

4. Does it really matter to you what your children become?

5. Do you feel pressure to turn your gifts into an enterprise of some sort?

Does God have a specific mission for me?

Not all of us can do great things. But we can do small things with great love.
—Mother Teresa[19]

LIKE I MENTIONED IN THE PREVIOUS CHAPTER, I CAN'T TELL you how many times I've wondered what exactly God wants me to do with my life, or how many times I've felt that I'm letting God down by going in a different direction than I suspect he originally planned for me. Many of us spend a fair bit of time guessing what God's plan for our life is and feeling great anxiety or guilt that we haven't quite figured it out yet. Again, I include myself here. Some people say follow your passions, while others say discover your gifts to reveal your ministry. Yet even after following advice such as this, and perhaps even after securing the ministry or the dream career we worked towards, we are still left wondering if this is what God has called us to do.

---

[19] Available at https://www.goodreads.com/author/quotes/838305.Mother_Teresa.

Speaking for myself, I have gone from working in youth ministry to apprenticing as a tradesman, then on to pursuing music and theatre, and now I work in law enforcement. I have explored my gifts, and I use them regularly, but I still wonder if I'm on the right path. Often, I question if I'm missing some great calling beyond my wildest dreams. Does God want me to become a prophet to the nations or continue in law enforcement? No matter what I choose to pursue, I still find myself questioning whether I'm following God's will.

After spending so much time worrying about this, I noticed within me some hidden motivation behind this question. It seemed that just beneath this humble willingness to serve God was also a great deal of craving for worldly recognition. I could see that when I asked God what he wanted me to do with my life, I was also asking him to will something for me that would make me great in the eyes of others. I wanted to be someone special. Everyone in this celebrity-crazed culture seems to believe that God has a *special* mission just for them. This hidden motivation may not be true for you, but it has been for me—and many, many others I've talked to about this. Refer back to St. Paul's quote in the previous chapter (Galatians 1:10).

Here is what I believe: God has the same mission for you as he does all his children, and if he wants you to do something different, more taxing, or utterly unique, he will absolutely find a way to let you know directly.

Maybe an example here will help. As a hockey coach, I have certain expectations for the members of the team. The players all understand that they must always do their best, show respect for themselves and others, listen to the coaches, and exhibit sportsmanship towards members of their own and opposing teams. The players don't approach me before each practice or game and ask me what my expectations are of them; they already know and understand what they are. They also recognize that I have those same expectations for all their other teammates.

During one Saturday morning practice, I was running a new drill. I knew that there were two players on the team that had above average skills that related to this drill. Before the practice, I approached these two players, one of them being my son Owen. I explained to my son and his teammate what I needed them to demonstrate for the rest of the team in the drill. Despite the doubt they both had concerning their ability to do this effectively, they did an exceptional job. They didn't boast of their special assignment to their teammates—they remained humble and understood that at times others would be leading them in drills in the same way.

If God has a specific mission for you, then like he did for prophets of the past, or I did for my son and his teammate, he will make that known to you in a very direct and obvious way. If not, it is practice as usual—only the expectations God has for us are a bit different. Live your best life, show love and respect for others and yourself, listen to and love God with all your heart, mind and soul, and be humble in service and recognition.

God has the same foundational mission for all of us, which can be discovered through his word in the scriptures, and if God has a specific mission that requires your unique gifts or talents, he will certainly call upon you directly. Until then, be part of the team and do your best.

At the end of every practice or game, I make every attempt to tell the whole team how much I appreciated their effort win or lose, and perhaps in the end the greatest coach of all will do the same for us as he modeled in Matthew 25:21 (RSV), saying *"Well done, good and faithful servant...."*

QUESTIONS TO PONDER

1. Do you get anxious when trying to discover God's will for your life?

2. What do you think God wants for you that he wants for all of us?

3. Do you feel that God has a special mission just for you, or can you accept that you are just part of the team like most others?

4. Does it make you feel anxious or leave you with a sense of relief to know that God has the same mission for most of us?

Does God favour the spiritually mature over the spiritual infant?

God loves each of us as if there were only one of us.
—Augustine[20]

I ONCE READ A QUOTE BY THE AUTHOR OF *THE PURPOSE Driven Life*, Rick Warren, that described God enjoying us at every moment of our spiritual development like earthly parents enjoy their children at all stages of their development. After each of my children were born, I always felt that the next ten to twelve months were the hardest for me. Change diapers, feed, bathe, cuddles followed by broken sleep. This continued morning until night. Maybe you had a different experience with your children, but I don't remember having many discussions with my children during these times. It was all about taking care of their basic needs and smothering them with affection. Even though there was not much reciprocal relationship in the form of conversation and shared interest, there was love; I could feel it, and I'm sure my three

---

[20] John R. Bodo, *Who They Really Were: Preaching on Biblical Personalities* (Lima, OH: CSS Publishing, 2000), p. 85.

children could feel it too. Despite this seemingly one-sided arrangement, I loved it.

When each of my children started walking I spent a lot of time chasing them, preventing falls, and redirecting their steps. My wife and I were constantly moving items out of their way so they could stumble around as safely as possible. This continued from morning until night, and we loved it. When my children started to talk and do small things for themselves, life changed yet again. There was a lot of picking up after them, cheering them on, re-brushing their teeth, cleaning up after their first attempt at making their own PB&J sandwich, and plenty of underwear changes. This continued morning until evening—and again, we loved it, and we were exhausted, and at times extremely stressed and frustrated.

All three of my children are now growing in stature and in vocabulary. This is both enlightening and frustrating. Our children now challenge us. They share with us; they make demands as well as small gestures of love. As they continue to grow, their unique personalities shine through, bringing with them unstated amounts of joy or exasperation. These days are much different than when they were infants or toddlers. These changes continue day to day and year to year from morning until night, hopefully for many more years, and I'm certain that my wife and I will still love it.

The point is that our love for our children is not dependant on what they can do for us. It is, in fact, not dependant on anything they do. It is shared with them simply because they were created out of love to be loved by us. My children do not have to earn my love; it is free and unconditional. Thus far, I have appreciated and loved every stage of their development, and I will continue to do so. Isn't it obvious that God would also love us at every stage of our relationship with him? Perhaps God enjoys a newly baptized infant just as much as a newly ordained priest. When my children were infants and couldn't get off their backs I carried them. When they began to crawl, I followed them closely. When they took their first steps, I was there to catch their many falls, and now that they walk by my side, I hold their hands. Is it possible that God does the same for all of us?

QUESTIONS TO PONDER

1. Do you remember loving your children more fully based on what age or stage of development they were at?

2. If you are not a parent, do you recall feeling more loved by your parents at any given age?

3. Do you consider yourself a spiritual infant or spiritually mature? Do you think it matters to God?

4. Think of the different ages and stages you went through with your children and how unique each was. What did you enjoy about each one in particular?

5. Do you see how God could enjoy each stage of your development in the same way?

How does God react to our anger?

*Father, forgive them;
for they know not what they do.*
(Luke 23:34, RSV)

THE BEDTIME ROUTINE AROUND OUR HOUSE USUALLY GOES rather smoothly. There is some protest and bargaining, but this is usually over quickly, and all three of the kids get tucked in and off to sleep before long.

One Sunday evening, my youngest son was having a particularly difficult time settling in. My wife laid down with him, but he was still crying, telling her that he was very angry with her for making him go to bed. It was my turn next. When I entered the room, he cried even more, telling me that we were both making him angry now. I attempted to lie down with him, but it didn't help him to calm down, so I asked him if he wanted some space. He said yes and I went off to prepare my lunch for work the next day. He continued to wail, and so I made my way back into the room. I asked if he needed a hug. He stood on his bed and wrapped his little arms around me. I picked him up and brought him to my reading chair in my room, where I rubbed his back until he calmed down. Within a short time, he was asleep.

The insight flashed. I noticed that the more upset my son became with me and the situation he felt I was responsible for, the more I desired to be closer to him. I wanted more than ever to comfort him, calm him, and assure him. I didn't argue with him or try to convince him that he didn't have a reason to be mad at me. Even though I knew his bedtime was justified and so was sending him to school the next day, I put that aside to just be with him. Doesn't God do the same for us?

When my son was lying with me on the chair, I started thinking of all the times in my own life I have been mad at God. I remembered being very angry with God many, many times, especially when family or friends were gravely ill, or when close friends lost a child to illness or in childbirth. I have spent many nights walking the streets, telling God how unfair I thought it was that young parents get sick and die, leaving behind their children, or that children die, leaving the parents with a hole in their hearts that never truly heals. On many of these occasions, I protested the randomness of life with its seemingly senseless tragedies and the all-out horror of diseases, natural disasters, and war. My anxiety would rise during these lamentations to God, and so would my anger. In the end, what I was really feeling was fear and separation, and I was lashing out at who I considered to be responsible for all this pain and anxiety. At times, I felt utterly betrayed and alone.

Even to this day, I still don't fully understand why God allows us to go through these things. Like my son Luke, I find myself telling God that he is making me angry—very angry, as

FROM ONE FATHER TO ANOTHER

a matter of fact. And just as my son did, I also try to push God away. He always comes back, though. He may give me space, but I'm sure he keeps a close eye on me—at least that's how I have felt during these outbursts of anger and frustration.

Is it possible that at these times, God understood my anger and fear—just as I had understood my son's—and only wished to comfort me and reassure me with his presence—that is, if I would let him?

If on that night I'd attempted to explain to my son why a certain number of hours of sleep were crucial for his health, or how school would only benefit him in the long run, I'm sure that wouldn't have calmed him in the moment; quite possibly, it would have overwhelmed him further. My son felt angry, afraid, and out of control. What he needed at that moment was me and all my presence. Perhaps when we feel overwhelmed, afraid, and angry, God offers us the same.

QUESTIONS TO PONDER

1. Can you think of times past or present when you have been angry with God?

2. Did you take these issues to God or push him away?

3. Do you feel that if God gave you a full explanation of why things are the way they are, you would be able to understand fully, or do you feel this would overwhelm you further?

4. What is it you need from God right now? Have you asked?

Can God be disappointed with us?

But God shows his love for us in that while we were yet sinners Christ died for us.
(Romans 5:8, RSV)

I WILL NEVER FORGET WATCHING AN INTERVIEW BETWEEN Dateline NBC's Stone Phillips and Jeffery Dahmer. On the small chance that you don't know who Dahmer is, he was a man who was deemed the "Milwaukee Monster" after he murdered and dismembered several young men during 1978–1991 in the Milwaukee area. Dahmer's father also sat in on this interview with Phillips. I'm still amazed that after all he knew about his son's actions and evil inclinations, he still chose to sit there with him—just as perplexed as the rest of us, yet still very much a father to his son. He sat there right beside him, and he supported his son with regular visits and honest attempts to understand the reasons behind his actions. How could he reconcile his love for his son with the utter vileness he inflicted on so many others?

There have been so many times that I have been disappointed by the actions of one of my children. Sometimes it was something they did to someone else, something hurtful they said, or even something they failed to do. Now obviously we are not talking about serial murder here, but I do think the illustration stands despite the distance in moral seriousness between Dahmer's actions and the actions of any one of my three children.

The important point here is that even when I may be disappointed with their actions, I never stop loving them. When my children hit each other or are caught in a lie, I can always separate who they are from what they have done. There are so many times in the scriptures where God expresses his disappointment with the actions of certain individuals. It has been said that God loves the sinner but hates the sin. King David is an appropriate example here, as well as some of Jesus' disciples. King David conspired to have the husband of the woman he lusted for murdered, and yet after all was said and done, David's great repentance led God to call him a man after his own heart. The disciples often quarrelled with one another, deserted Jesus, denied knowing him, and one disciple, as we know, ultimately betrayed him. Jesus still loved them all.

God can certainly be disappointed in our actions—he most likely is disappointed on most days—and yet always loves us the same way we do with our own children. God can separate the sin from the sinner just as you and I can (or may have to do in the future) with our own children. I'm not sure what mistakes my children will make, although some of them surely will be trivial compared to others; however, I want my children to know that even when they mess up, act out of maliciousness, or fail in any number of moral decisions, that they are not necessarily screw-ups, entirely evil, or complete failures. I want my children to know that they are loved, no matter what they do, even though I may be very disappointed in what they choose or how they act. They will understand that I choose to love them always. They will also understand that because of my love for them, I enforce consequences and allow natural effects to follow their choices, as I discussed in an earlier chapter. Is it possible that God feels and acts the same? That being said, these consequences can be very serious in nature, ultimately affecting where we will spend eternity. We explore this in the next chapter.

QUESTIONS TO PONDER

1. Can you remember a time when you were deeply disappointed with one of your children?

2. Can you see that it was because of your love for them that you were disappointed?

3. Do you feel that God is disappointed with you?

4. Can you accept that God loves you despite all your shortcomings?

5. What do you think God wants you to understand about his love for you?

Will God send his children to hell?

...because the Lord disciplines those he loves, as a father the son he delights in.
(Proverbs 3:12, NIV)

DOLING OUT PUNISHMENT FOR MY CHILDREN IS ALWAYS difficult, even if it's justified. Punishing them forever is unfathomable to me; nonetheless, this is what we are told may happen to some of God's children. The word "hell" conjures up all kinds of horrible images—haunting scenes like unquenchable fire, tormented souls, and utter blackness, to name just a few. Even if these images are metaphorical or inaccurate, the idea that hell is not a very nice place seems most certain. Even Jesus tells us this in Matthew 13:50 (NIV): *"...and throw them into the blazing furnace, where there will be weeping and gnashing of teeth."*

How a loving God could allow any of his beloved children to go to a place that has any amount of torment, suffering, or eternal struggle is a tough sell to anyone, myself included. At times, I struggle to punish my children for much more than a few hours (or days in some of the more serious cases). To be honest, I wasn't even sure I wanted to write this chapter, thinking that I couldn't provide any insight that would satisfy me emotionally or logically, let alone anyone else. Knowing that a place like hell exists and is sanctioned by a loving God can be extremely hard to reconcile, but maybe, in the end, this is not entirely unreasonable or unjust.

Considering that none of my three children have done anything warranting a prison sentence, I know that using them as an example might not fly in this case. Rather, I will appeal to the sense of justice we share as human beings. Rarely do you hear someone saying that they don't think Hitler should be punished for what he did during World War II; in fact, you hear people say things like "I hope he rots in hell" or "Surely, hell was created for people like Hitler." When Saddam Hussein, Osama Bin Laden, or Timothy McVeigh were brought to justice, whether they were imprisoned or executed, there weren't many people that accused the authorities of being evil or unjust for punishing them. When child killers like John Wayne Gacy or serial killers like Russell Williams or Ted Bundy are sentenced to life in prison without the chance for parole, we generally do not take their side and demand their release—yet we accuse God of being unjust for punishing the likes of these people just the same.

It is important to reflect on whether you agree that life sentences imposed on criminals like Gacy or Bundy make sense and are just. When I reflect on this question, I realize that not only do I want these people to pay for their crimes, I also don't want them to be able to commit further offences. We want them kept from ever hurting or killing another person again. I think you would agree that we want all people like them to be caught and "put away for good."

Does God allow some of his children to go to hell as a final sentence? I think he does, and for the same reasons just mentioned: to punish their crimes and to keep them from continuing to hurt his other children. Does that mean God does this without a heavy heart? I don't think so. Although I punish my children at times, I have never doled out punishment or enforced a consequence with a smile on my face; in fact, I'm more likely to feel my heart breaking in those times, as small as they may be. My favourite moments are when one of my children realizes their mistake and asks for forgiveness or offers to make it right. Doesn't God feel the same way? I think he does—but that doesn't mean he forgoes consequences, especially if repentance is not genuine and forgiveness is not sought.

I realize that I am comparing the innocent sins of children with the monstrous sins of serial murderers and terrorists. Well, I have arrested many people throughout my career. Some arrests were made for minor infractions while others were for much more serious offences. Many times, I have had to attend court and testify to the facts of the case to ensure that the consequences for the accused are warranted and fair in their severity. Some cases end with the convicted paying a small fine, while others can end in jail time or even a prison sentence. Doesn't God treat sin in the same way? Perhaps God also considers the case and has different levels of consequences for different levels of sin. Mathew 12:31 (ESV) speaks to this when Jesus is quoted as saying, *"Therefore I tell you, every sin and blasphemy will be forgiven, but the blasphemy against the Spirit will not be forgiven."* God clearly deems some sins greater than others, and I'm sure the punishment coming from a loving, compassionate and just God always fits the crime. All sin separates us from God, but perhaps different sins separate us to a lesser or greater degree (partly because of the level of shame we feel).

Depending on what wrongdoing my children commit, I also "consider the case." If one of my children decides to leave their homework at school on purpose, I am disappointed; however, if one of them happens to hurt their brother or sister intentionally, I am both disappointed and angry at their actions to a higher degree. Both scenarios would elicit a different consequence in severity as well. In relation to the homework being left at school, I would enforce a consequence to correct the behaviour of my child. In the case of one of my children intentionally injuring their sibling, I impose consequences because I wish to correct the error of my child's actions towards their sibling, but at the same time, I want to offer a sense of justice to the child that was hurt. Doesn't God also have these two objectives in mind when he imposes punishment on his children?

Now, no matter what my children do, if they genuinely feel remorse and turn to me for forgiveness, I am always willing to help them move past their mistakes. However, what happens when our children grow into young adults and their actions go beyond a simple infraction, maybe even evolving to the criminal or monstrous? We can use the actions of young mass shooters here as an example, or child predators, or yes, even serial killers. What do we do then?

As difficult as it is to imagine, we must ask ourselves what we would do if one of our children were to commit crimes such as Bundy, McVeigh, Gacy, or Aileen Wuornos did. Would you

FROM ONE FATHER TO ANOTHER

let them off the hook if they said sorry and promised not to do it again? Because of your unconditional love for your child, you would most likely want to accept their apology, be done with it, and make them feel better. You would also want them to know that you can hate the sin they committed and still love them deeply. What loving parent wouldn't want their child to feel the same? However, I don't think you would be okay with them walking away scot free. As painful as it is to admit, you would know in the depths of your heart that if you or a loved one became a victim of such sins as a result of the actions of another person's child, you would be experiencing the hunger pains of justice as well. Think back to the interview I mentioned between Jeffrey Dahmer, his dad, and Stone Phillips. Dahmer's father still loved his son very much despite his heinous actions, but that's not to say that he condoned Jeffrey's actions in any way. I don't think it's even possible to consider that he did, but he did realize that there was a higher justice that had to be fulfilled, regardless of his wish to forgive his son and restore him back to the innocent child he once was. Mr. Dahmer knew that his son had a penalty to pay for his crimes, and he painfully admitted that the sentence was just and fair.

That's the point. If we think of Hitler being in hell, most of us don't suffer too much sympathy for him, especially if you have taken the time to hear some of the testimonies of concentration camp survivors, and even more so, the stories and images of the ones who didn't survive, including small children who were ushered into gas chambers wailing and calling out for their mothers and fathers.

The higher justice in Dahmer's case was the human law. The higher justice we are speaking of here is God. God is justice—his very nature is justice and love. As offensive as this next statement may sound to some people, it nevertheless remains true. God loves Dahmer, Gacy, and Williams. He loves them like he loves you and me, but because of their (free will) transgressions, his nature demands that justice be served, not only to punish their transgressions, but to also provide a sense of justice for their victims. Essentially, people like Dahmer and Gacy choose hell by not choosing to follow God's law, and God allows the consequences to follow.

Can't we see that we accuse God of being unjust when he exacts the very justice we demand? Can't we see that God is protecting heaven from the rebellious souls of hell? How would you react if, after convicting Gacy of his many murders, the judge released him back into society? To me, this seems like what we are asking God to do when we argue against hell. Many of us support life sentences in certain cases, and then accuse God of evil when he does the same!

I had to ask myself how I would feel if I did in fact make it to heaven one day and Hitler was there enjoying the fruits of heaven with Gacy. This scenario brings up many conflicting emotions. On one hand, I don't want to see anyone suffer hell, but on the other hand, I want to know that the narrow road I tried to travel leads somewhere that the wide road does not. I want to know that the struggle against my narcissism, rage, and lust, as well as my efforts towards temperance meant something to God. It is my hope that my continued repentance for my sins will be a worthwhile act, worthy in the eyes of God. When all is said and done, what I'm really asking for is justice. Aren't you hoping for the same?

Just as we punish our children for their sins, small and large and in different degrees, can't we see how God would do the same? And just as no loving parent wants to see their child suffer consequences permanently, God does not want any of his children to be separated from him in hell. As a father, I can always appeal to my own sense of justice to discipline and enforce consequences for my own children, but it is not in my power to deal out an acceptable sentence if they were to be guilty of murder or rape. In this case, I would have to appeal to a higher law and accept that the punishment may be something severe as life in prison.

God is the highest law, and he has the authority to sanction eternal life in hell. Keep in mind that God did not choose this—we did, through our actions and rejection of God's grace. As C.S. Lewis once said, "...there are only two types of people in the end. Those who say to God, 'Thy will be done, and those to whom God says in the end, 'Thy will be done.'"[21] Amazingly, God provided a way for this not to happen. He provided a way for us to avoid hell, despite standing convicted as guilty in our sins. Even more amazingly, he did this for people like Williams and McVeigh just as much as for you and me.

God's nature may demand justice, but that does not prevent him from deciding how that justice is satisfied. You can leave this world shaking your fist at God such as famous atheists Christopher Hitchens did, or you can decide to ask God to receive you in his mercy, which he made possible through his gift of grace. The choice is yours. How God did this, we will visit in the next chapter.

---

[21] Quoted in *Who Made God?: And Answers to over 100 other Tough Questions of Faith*, Ravi Zacharias & Norman Geisler, eds. (Grand Rapids, MI: Zondervan, 2009), p. 30.

QUESTIONS TO PONDER

1. Do you agree that some crimes deserve life sentences? Why or why not?

2. How do you "consider the case" when it comes to punishing your children?

3. If one of your children were to commit murder, orchestrate a mass shooting, or rape someone, would you accept that they might serve a life sentence?

4. Are there any crimes you have heard of or can think of that would warrant God sending someone to hell?

5. Do you think everyone should be in heaven? Why or why not?

6. Do you feel that God's gift of grace applies to you, and do you accept it?

Why does God have to pay our debt?

For the wages of sin is death, but the free gift of God is eternal life in Christ Jesus our Lord.
(Romans 6:23, RSV)

GOD PAYING OUR DEBT TO HIMSELF. HUH? I HAVE ALWAYS struggled with the idea of God sending his son to suffer and die for us when he could have decided to let it all go himself. Besides, we are accountable to him and he is not accountable to anyone outside of himself. Why doesn't God just let it all go? Probably because he can't—and not because he wants to and some force outside himself does not allow him to. This would be saying in effect that God is governed by a force existing outside of and greater than Him. This is not the case— Revelation 22:13 (RSV) says, *"I am the Alpha and the Omega, the first and the last, the beginning and the end."* Justice does not exist without God. His very nature is to be just, and so his nature demands it. Let's try to clarify this.

It's hard to come up with actual examples where my children have had me step up to pay a debt for them that wouldn't sound trite, like fixing the broken window of a neighbour or replacing a toy belonging to one of their friends. We sometimes must do these things to make things right with neighbour; however, what we are talking about here is much more serious than a broken window or toy. Because of the heaviness of the issue presented, I will speak hypothetically to illustrate this point, as I did in the previous chapter on hell.

Imagine one day one of your children decides to drink and drive, and this choice ultimately leads to a major collision resulting in the death of another person. As horrible as this situation is, it is unfortunately a reality for many. Now imagine a time weeks or months after the collision, when your son or daughter stands before a judge and is convicted of the crime and sentenced harshly with time in jail or prison.

Can you imagine what you would be feeling? The child is now placed in handcuffs and turns to you, pleading; utter fear and despair are evident on their face, and tears are streaming down their cheeks. Even though your son or daughter is now considered a grown man or woman, all you see is your child calling out to you for help because they are entirely unable to help themselves. There is obvious remorse on their part, but the consequences go hand in hand with the crime, and there is nothing that you can do. In fact, standing across the courtroom are the mother and father who lost their own daughter in the collision. Their presence forces you to agree that the penalty must be paid, despite how painful that admission is. You are stunned and deeply saddened.

Just as the court officers are about to lead your child away, the judge stops and calls attention to the court. The judge looks at your child, explaining that he can sense genuine remorse on their part. The judge wishes the whole thing had never happened, and expresses his anguish about all the young life falling in ruins. He affirms that the punishment imposed is just.

You feel like your feet are sinking into the ground, and that you might faint. And at that moment all the love you have for your child wells up in your chest and you stand and blurt out apprehensively, "Please, your honour—let me take the place of my child. I will pay the penalty!"

The courtroom is unsettled, and the judge has to a call for order. This judge is known to be the fairest kind, and yet thoroughly an adherent and protector of the law. In the silence and confusion that follows, the judge stares intently. He appears to be considering this option and is clearly moved by compassion, as a single tear on his cheek betrays.

The judge turns to the parents whose daughter was killed. This mother and father are also moved to tears as they have a sudden realization that alongside the hate and the wish for retribution in their hearts, there is also compassion for the convicted. They remember that their own daughter had made the very same mistake of drinking and driving in the past, but without the dire consequences faced this day. The two sets of parents suddenly embrace in a flood of emotion as they realize their common bond in unconditional love for their children.

After some time, the father of the girl that lost her life steps forward and petitions the judge that your precious child be set free, and that you also be freed from paying any penalty. Through tears, this man explains that he feels there is enough remorse on your child's part and that he forgives the crime and the debt to his family.

The judge once again appears to consider the option. The judge then explains that that his court is in fact one of justice and that the law must be kept. He again affirms that the punishment is just. Many moments of deafening silence pass. The judge then places his gavel back on his bench gently. For you, the silence is broken only by the thumping in your ears as your heart pumps more and more forcefully, waiting for your child to be led away.

Just then, the judge leaves his bench and slowly makes his way to stand in front of the gathering of the court. There, he removes his robes and extends his hands to the court officer. The judge looks at your child in the eyes, saying that he himself will accept the punishment and pay the penalty. The gasps are anything but silent. The judge silences the court and tells those gathered that he will not change the law or the demands of justice, but that he does have the authority and discretion to determine how those demands are fulfilled in his own court. The crowd continues to stir restlessly, whispering to one another in shock and disbelief.

As the judge is lead away, he turns to your child, asking if the gift he is offering is accepted. Your child is moved to tears, and falls to their knees feeling unworthy, remorseful, and thankful all at once. Once your child affirms the covenant, the judge then tells your child to leave the courthouse in peace, reassuring everyone that the penalty has been paid.

Obviously, this fictitious scenario is far from fact, but its underlying theme of vicarious atonement is exactly what God the ultimate judge did for us in Jesus Christ his son. The differences between the human judge and God are many—the major difference being that the human judge is subject to the law of the courts, while God *is* the law. God is the source of morality, not an adherent to it. In the above story, the human judge forgives one subject of one crime because that is his jurisdiction within his court here on earth; God's jurisdiction is the whole human race and his court is all creation.

Of course, there would have been protests in the courtroom our story took place in, and probably riots, because we can always argue and disagree with a human decision and appeal it. Some would say that the judge cannot take the place of the convicted, and that it doesn't make any sense. Others judges surely would appeal the decision to avoid precedent. But with God there is no appeal after a decision is made, and there are no other judges. God chose to change the way the demands of justice were satisfied by satisfying them himself through Jesus. Who can appeal the superior judge, or in our human system of justice, the superior court? It is a final decision. God chose to step down from his bench, and instead of extending his hands for the cuffs of the court officer like the judge in this story, he extended his arms for the Roman guard's nails.

In the above scenario, the convicted child could have refused the judge's vicarious offering, therefore leaving them once again shouldering their own consequences and burdens. In the end, all the convicted had to do was accept the judge's offering to pay the penalty himself and then be set free. Doesn't God ask the same from us? God asks us to accept what he did through Jesus—and what does he ask of us in return but for a contrite heart and a willingness to repent from sin and change our ways? If we do accept and repent, we too can walk out of the courthouse—completely guilty as charged, and yet free.

So why did God have to pay our debt? Well, he didn't. He chose to because he was moved by his love and compassion for us. He did this freely, just as the human judge in our story did. The human judge was moved by the tremendous and genuine remorse on the part of the convicted person, and decided that even though making the guilty individual pay the penalty was a just requirement of the law, he didn't want to see that person suffer those consequences and live their whole natural life in prison. This is how God sees the situation. God does not want to see us suffer the consequences of sin in our daily lives, so if we genuinely repent and work to change, he steps in and pays the penalty. He does this out of love and compassion for his children! Do you accept?

Does heaven exist?

My Father's house has many rooms; if that were not so, would I have told you that I am going there to prepare a place for you?
(John 14:2, NIV)

I'VE NEVER BEEN TO NEW YORK OR SWITZERLAND, AND I'VE never been to heaven either. I can't tell you what heaven is like, and personally I don't know of anyone who can, although I do think the descriptions given by people who have had near-death experiences might offer some clues. What I can tell you is this: I believe that heaven is an actual place and is as real as New York or Switzerland. I also don't believe this conviction is engaging in some form of wish fulfillment based on fantasy, either; it is based on the very desires I find within me. C.S. Lewis once said that, "If we find ourselves with a desire that nothing in this world can satisfy, then the most probable explanation is that we were made for another world."[22] Lewis

---
[22] Available at https://www.goodreads.com/quotes/363092-if-i-find-in-myself-desires-which-nothing-in-this.

explained that as human beings, we never discover within us a desire that does not have the possibility of satisfaction, but we do find desires that cannot be satisfied in this world. Here on earth, if we are hungry there is food; for thirst, water; for love, relationship; and for hunger of knowledge, truth, to name just a few—but we also find that we have the desire for God and eternity in our hearts and on our minds that cannot be fully satisfied here on earth, hence Lewis's quote. Ecclesiastes 3:11 (NIV) also affirms this: *"He has also set eternity in the human heart...."* Well, among other things, I do find in myself the wish and the longing to be close with God and live forever. It follows that God and eternity would be the corresponding experiences that can satisfy these desires, doesn't it?

As simple as this sounds, I challenge you to put Lewis' insight to the test by considering what longings you find within your soul and body and then asking if there are any that seem to not have the possibility of satisfaction. I'm willing to bet that you won't find any orphan desires within. I think you will see that for every desire within you there is a corresponding experience that leads to the fulfillment (whether immediate or eventual) of that longing. I have not yet been able to discover a desire or wish within me that is left wanting with no corresponding experience to satisfy it. It seems that we were not created with craving and desires that must forever remain wanting. I come to this truth through experience, not by some theory or esoteric philosophy. This is what I find within myself; perhaps it rings true for you as well.

Like most people, I may not have an accurate portrait of what heaven will be like, but I do think this world dimly reflects what's to come in the many rooms Jesus refers to in John

14:2, albeit in larger and more refined forms of beauty than we find here. What I can imagine is a place of no death, no suffering, no unfulfilled desires, total acceptance, complete justice, and the assurance of being closer with God. I have had atheist friends of mine say to me that heaven sounds just like a fantasy world. I would have to agree with them. Heaven *is* a fantasy—one where all that we desire is satisfied and all wrongs are made right. In saying that, a little reflection would show that most of us spend much of our time on this earth trying to avoid suffering, experience unconditional love, find peace of mind, tip the scales of justice, and be closer to God. When all is said and done, we are all trying to find heaven here on earth, even at this moment. Could it be said then, that we are engaging in fantastical thinking on a daily basis? Why is the idea of heaven so easily written off as fantasy then? It just so happens that heaven *does* provide the experiences and satisfaction of our deepest desires and most fervent wishes, and that makes perfect sense to me. Why else would we strive for them if they could not be attained? Again, where in nature do you find other creatures frustrated in their desires? Do frogs wish to bark? Do horses wish to fly? It seems that each creature is endowed with unique desires, urges, and instincts that lead that creature to the best possible existence for themselves—one where they will be satisfied. Why should we be any different?

Just because we have wishes that seem too good to be true, it does not in any way entail that what we wish for cannot or does not exist. As humans, we wish for all sorts of things in our lives that seem too good to be true, but nevertheless turn out to be the happy ending we always dreamed of. Imagine a single person holding out the wish that one day they will meet someone special that they can spend the rest of their life with, or imagine a small child in an orphanage who wishes and dreams one day to be chosen and loved by people they can call their family. If we decided that all wishes that seem too good to be true are therefore fantasy, then most of us would lose all hope rather quickly. Might I add that many of us *are* in fact living the wishes we made in the past that once seemed more fantasy than reality. The fact is that often our wishes do come true, no matter how much of a fantasy they may seem to be. People do find a special person to spend their lives with; small children do find families that choose to love them (like my friend Piero wrote about in the foreword of this book). Wishes do come true, because wishes start with desire, and desires lead to the satisfaction or fulfillment of those very wishes, either on this side of heaven or in heaven to come. In 1 Corinthians 2:9 (NIV), St. Paul reminds us that it will be beyond anything we can imagine: *"'What no eye has seen, what no ear has heard, and what no human mind has conceived'—the things God has prepared for those who love him..."*

I will end this chapter with a hypothetical scenario between my children and me. Imagine that one day I brought my kids to the park. This park has a few swings, a rather worn-out jungle gym, and a splash pad that is only half functioning, but despite this, they have fun anyway. After all, it's still the park, and there are still plenty of things to do to keep them amused. After a short time, I try to get my kids to leave, telling them I have somewhere else I want to take them, but they don't want to leave. They insist that I tell them where I plan on taking them, protesting that it can't be better than the park. They refuse to believe my assurances that they will love my

FROM ONE FATHER TO ANOTHER

planned destination much more than the park. I try to explain that although it will have some similarities to the park, the new experience will be much more exhilarating and wonderful. Even though my kids are making it difficult for me to get them to leave the park, I feel that this just makes the surprise I have in store for them that much better, because what my kids don't know is that very night we have a plane to catch to Disneyland. You might ask, why not just come out and tell them? Well, because the excitement of a surprise arrival would provide even more joy for them.

Is it possible God feels the same about heaven? Perhaps it's true that what God has in store for us is in fact much greater than any eye has seen or any ear has heard, and undoubtedly the most fervent desires we experience here on earth are really nothing more or less than a desire for God and heaven.

QUESTIONS TO PONDER

1. Can you see that within you there is no hunger that cannot be satisfied?

2. Reflect on what heaven would fulfill for you. Do you find that you spend much of your time trying to attain those very things here on earth?

3. Do you trust that God has prepared a place for the ones that love him that is beyond comprehension?

4. If you struggle to believe that heaven is an actual place, why do you think that is?

5. Can you imagine that heaven would be as different from earth as a neighbourhood park would be to Disneyland?

6. What desires do you have that can only be satisfied by heaven?

Afterword

I MENTIONED AT THE BEGINNING OF THIS BOOK THAT, IN THE end, I was probably writing more for myself than for others, in the hope of gaining a deeper understanding of God's character and intentions. But I do hope it got you thinking as well. I also hopefully made it clear that no metaphor can explain anything fully. However, some of the answers God led me to throughout this process have satisfied me intellectually, even if my emotions at times still protest through pangs of hunger.

As time goes on and I enter new phases of relationship with my children, I can be sure that new challenges will arise, and with them, conceivably, more insights will come to light in my journey to understand God. Isaiah 55:8–9 (RSV) tells us that God's ways are not our ways and his thoughts are higher than ours. Being a parent of a four-year-old right now, I can understand why God would say that. I don't expect to understand every action, inaction, reason, or process God employs in the running of a universe. St. Paul's letter to the Romans 9:20 basically reminds us not to let our egos get away from us here.

At some point during the writing of this book, I realized that I could just keep writing more and more as different scenarios played out in my life with my children and new insights presented themselves. I decided that I would stop where I did and add another volume, if warranted, sometime in the future. There are days when I'm certain God is with me in my life, and other days when I'm not so sure at all. Most days my children trust me. I trust God most days as well, but on others I feel God is being unfair, intentionally distant, or the very opposite of caring. It is at these times that I reflect on my own love for my children and how they may have perceived the very same things about me occasionally when I'm busy, away for work, or perhaps imposing a consequence. Despite these erroneous observations on my children's part, my love for each of them has never changed, nor have I forgotten my care for every single hair on their precious heads.

As this has been a book of questions, I will end with a question as well, the same question I have been asking throughout this book: is it possible that God feels the same?